AF226397

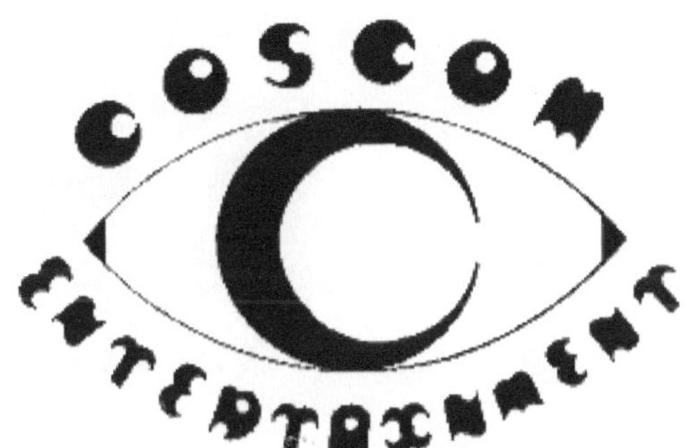
COSCOM
ENTERTAINMENT

ALSO BY A.P. FUCHS

BLOOD OF MY WORLD TRILOGY

DISCOVERY OF DEATH
MEMORIES OF DEATH
LIFE OF DEATH

UNDEAD WORLD TRILOGY

BLOOD OF THE DEAD
POSSESSION OF THE DEAD
REDEMPTION OF THE DEAD

THE AXIOM-MAN™ SAGA
(LISTED IN READING ORDER)

AXIOM-MAN
EPISODE NO. 0: FIRST NIGHT OUT
DOORWAY OF DARKNESS
EPISODE NO. 1: THE DEAD LAND
CITY OF RUIN
OF MAGIC AND MEN (COMIC BOOK)

OTHER FICTION

A STRANGER DEAD
A RED DARK NIGHT
APRIL (WRITING AS PETER FOX)
MAGIC MAN (DELUXE CHAPBOOK)
THE WAY OF THE FOG (THE ARK OF LIGHT VOL. 1)
DEVIL'S PLAYGROUND (WRITTEN WITH KEITH GOUVEIA)
ON HELL'S WINGS (WRITTEN WITH KEITH GOUVEIA)
ZOMBIE FIGHT NIGHT: BATTLES OF THE DEAD
MAGIC MAN PLUS 15 TALES OF TERROR
UNDENIABLE

ANTHOLOGIES (AS EDITOR)

DEAD SCIENCE
ELEMENTS OF THE FANTASTIC
VICIOUS VERSES AND REANIMATED RHYMES: ZANY ZOMBIE POETRY
FOR THE UNDEAD HEAD
METAHUMANS VS THE UNDEAD
BIGFOOT TERROR TALES VOL. 1 (WITH ERIC S. BROWN)
BIGFOOT TERROR TALES VOL. 2 (WITH ERIC S. BROWN)
METAHUMANS VS WEREWOLVES

NON-FICTION

BOOK MARKETING FOR THE
FINANCIALLY-CHALLENGED AUTHOR
CANADIAN SCRIBBLER: COLLECTED LETTERS OF AN
UNDERGROUND WRITER
LOOK, UP ON THE SCREEN! THE BIG BOOK OF
SUPERHERO MOVIE REVIEWS

POETRY

THE HAND I'VE BEEN DEALT
HAUNTED MELODIES AND OTHER DARK POEMS
STILL ABOUT A GIRL

GO TO

WWW.CANISTERX.COM

&

WWW.AXIOM-MAN.COM

LOOK, UP ON THE SCREEN!

THE *BIG* BOOK OF SUPERHERO MOVIE REVIEWS

A.P. FUCHS

COSCOM ENTERTAINMENT
WINNIPEG

ISBN 978-1-927339-48-0

Movie runtime data researched at www.imdb.com

Published by COSCOM ENTERTAINMENT
www.coscomentertainment.com

A.P. FUCHS website: www.canisterx.com

Text set in Garamond; Printed and Bound in the USA

For my wife, Roxanne, who lets me stay up late to watch movies and buy superhero DVDs without question.

Sometimes she even makes the popcorn.

The Reel

Origin 1

The Reviews:

All-Star Superman (2011) 4
Amazing Spider-Man, The (2012) 6
Avengers, The (2012) 8
Batman (1966) 11
Batman (1989) 13
Batman & Robin (1997) 15
Batman and Mr. Freeze: SubZero (1998) 16
Batman Begins (2005) 18
Batman Beyond: Return of the Joker (2000) 20
Batman Forever (1995) 21
Batman: Gotham Knight (2008) 23
Batman: Mask of the Phantasm (1993) 26
Batman: Mystery of the Batwoman (2003) 28
Batman Returns (1992) 30
Batman vs Dracula, The (2005) 31
Batman: Year One (2011) 32
Blade (1998) 34
Blade II (2002) 36
Blade: Trinity (2004) 38
Blankman (1994) 40
Captain America (1990) 42
Captain America: The First Avenger (2011) 44
Catwoman (2004) 46
Chronicle (2012) 48
Daredevil (2003) 50
Dark Knight, The (2008) 52
Dark Knight Rises, The (2012) 55
Defendor (2009) 57
Elektra (2005) 59
Fantastic 4: Rise of the Silver Surfer (2007) 61
Fantastic Four (2005) 63
Ghost Rider (2007) 65
Green Hornet, The (2011) 66

Green Lantern (2011) 68
Green Lantern: First Flight (2009) 70
Hancock (2008) 72
Hellboy (2004) 74
Hellboy II: The Golden Army (2008) 76
Hero at Large (1980) 78
Hulk (2003) 79
Hulk vs (2009) 81
Incredible Hulk, The (2008) 83
Incredibles, The (2004) 85
Invincible Iron Man, The (2007) 88
Iron Man (2008) 89
Iron Man 2 (2010) 91
Iron Man 3 (2013) 93
Iron Monkey (1993/2001) 95
Justice League: Crisis on Two Earths (2010) 97
Justice League: Doom (2012) 99
Justice League: The Flashpoint Paradox (2013) 101
Justice League: The New Frontier (2008) 103
Kick-Ass (2010) 105
Legend of Zorro, The (2005) 107
LEGO Batman: The Movie – DC Superheroes Unite! (2013) 109
Look, Up in the Sky! The Amazing Story of Superman (2006) 111
Man of Steel (2013) 112
Mask of Zorro, The (1998) 115
Meteor Man, The (1993) 117
My Super Ex-girlfriend (2006) 119
Mystery Men (1999) 121
Phantom, The (1996) 123
Planet Hulk (2010) 125
Punisher, The (2004) 127
Rocketeer, The (1991) 129
Shadow, The (1994) 130
Sky High (2005) 131
Spawn (1997) 133
Spider-Man (2002) 135
Spider-Man 2 (2004) 137
Spider-Man 3 (2007) 139
Spirit, The (2008) 142
Supergirl (1984) 144
Superhero Movie (2008) 146

Superman (1978) 148
Superman II (1980) 151
Superman II: The Richard Donner Cut (2006) 153
Superman III (1983) 155
Superman IV: The Quest for Peace (1987) 157
Superman/Batman: Apocalypse (2010) 159
Superman/Batman: Public Enemies (2009) 161
Superman: Brainiac Attacks (2006) 163
Superman: Doomsday (2007) 165
Superman Returns (2006) 167
Superman: Unbound (2013) 169
Superman vs the Elite (2012) 171
Thor (2011) 173
Ultimate Avengers: The Movie (2006) 175
Ultimate Avengers 2: Rise of the Panther (2006) 177
Unbreakable (2000) 178
V for Vendetta (2005) 180
Watchmen: Tales of the Black Freighter & Under the Hood (2009) . . 182
Watchmen: The Ultimate Cut (2009) 184
Wraith: Eyes of Judgment, The (2005) 186
X2: X-Men United (2003) 188
X-Men (2000) 190
X-Men: First Class (2011) 192
X-Men: The Last Stand (2006) 194
X-Men Origins: Wolverine (2009) 196
Zoom (2006) 198

Origin
by
A.P. Fuchs

This whole book started by accident.

Kinda.

You see, six years ago I wanted to come up with a way to get more people to my website and so thought doing movie reviews would be a cool way to do that. And what movies do I love the most? Superhero ones, of course. I think I wrote three or four in a row that afternoon, and when you're a stay-at-home dad with a one-year-old who was active as all get out, writing three or four reviews straight is nothing to sneeze at. Did them longhand, too.

Anyway, I kept up with it for a while and posted them on my site, then other things would come up and I'd be writing something else, whether fiction, comics or just general blog posts. Over the years, I wrote movie reviews when I could and posted them shortly thereafter, and while I also did reviews for horror flicks, sci-fi, mockumentaries and others, superhero movies made up most of my review list.

A few years ago I stumbled upon the world of movie review books—can you believe I didn't know they existed in the number that they do?—and while I knew of Leonard Maltin's mammoth books, I didn't know others had written them as well. I somehow came across a series of review books by Tim Gross who runs the *Gross Movie Reviews* website and publishes a series of review books of the same name. I picked up his first one and really enjoyed it. He does his reviews much differently than mine, but they're a lot of fun nonetheless.

Speaking of which, when I first started reviewing movies, I really didn't know what I was doing and, well, there are tons of ways to review movies, everything from a brief paragraph like Tim does all the way to long drawn-out essays on the different aspects of a flick. I know my first batch of reviews were perhaps overly analytical, and I felt I needed to review the story, the music, the performances and more for each and every review. And while I still review those things, I don't have a checklist on what does or what does not need to part of my reviews. In the end, I write them as if I'm just talking about them, what I liked, what I didn't, and also insert a few [hopefully] interesting asides along the way.

You'll probably pick up on that as you read these, that is, the changes in style as the reviews weren't written in alphabetical order like they are presented here.

The thing with reviewing movies, I've learned, is I have to remark on them for what they are and for when they were made, especially superhero flicks. You can't go and review *Man of Steel* then review *Batman* from 1966 through the same lens. Each have their merits, each have their faults, and each should be judged on their own for what they were and/or for what they were intended to be. To hold each of them to the same standard would be unfair since superhero movie standards have changed over time. Right now, we're enjoying a golden age of superhero cinema, with a half dozen or more superhero movies coming out each year, whether on the big screen or small. In ten years, I'm sure my feelings for the movies are going to change and what we view as awesome superhero cinema now might not be so cool then. Or maybe the latest crop of super flicks will hold up. There's no way to know until we get there.

As a fan, the reviews within are reviewed through a fan's lens, and likewise they're reviewed through the lens of someone who writes fiction for a living, a good chunk of which is superhero fiction (*The Axiom-man Saga*). I know that it takes a great deal of work just to write and publish a book, a lot of love, a lot of thought, a lot of trial and error, and while creating a book and creating a movie are different, there are similarities in regards to writing good characters, the presentation of the idea for the story, the effort to create under pressure, and so on. That said, I'm not one to ever say something sucks or to give something a one-star review because it's not my cup of tea. In my opinion, no creative effort is ever worth one star. Every book I read, every song I've heard, every movie I've seen, while they might not all be "my thing," and while some really just aren't that good or interesting, each still had at least one thing that made it fun or entertaining or made me think or whatnot and that counts for something, so you won't find any one-star reviews in this book.

The review system is based on a five-star rating. Ratings are given for different reasons, quality of movie only being one of them. Some of these flicks are from my childhood and so sentimental value plays a part in awarding what could be argued as overly-generous positive merits in some cases. Some flicks have dumb stories but are meant to be funny so are graded on that. They are also rated in this book as what I thought about them at the time of review. Some of my feelings toward them have changed since, but I left them as written for the sake of giving an honest snapshot of what I thought about them at point of review.

As a fair warning, while the reviews are mostly spoiler free, there are some that reveal a few things so I'm giving you a friendly heads up on that now. If you haven't seen a movie I've reviewed here and don't want to know anything about it, then skip over that review and read the next one.

Compiling this book has shown me there is a ton of superhero cinema out there. It's one thing to kind of know that or acknowledge it, but another to see it firsthand when you're putting together the table of contents and adding up how many hours of superhero entertainment you've watched. (And this is just the movies never mind all the superhero TV shows I've seen, too.)

I've chosen one hundred reviews for this book so if there's a superhero movie that is not reviewed here, chances are it'll be in the next batch of one hundred reviews for volume two.

Bottom line? I love superhero movies. They're awe-inspiring, heart-inspiring, motivating, and are just a great time, even the worst of them.

What you are about to read are one lifelong fanboy's opinion on superhero movies and what he thought of them. I hope you enjoy it.

Cheers.

A.P. Fuchs
July-August, 2013
Winnipeg, MB

All-Star Superman (2011)
Written by Dwayne McDuffie
Directed by Sam Liu
Runtime 76 min.
5 out of 5

The Man of Steel is dying after receiving an extreme dose of solar radiation. Trying to live out his last days and wrap up all loose ends, he spends it with Lois and gives her a special serum that grants her superpowers for twenty-four hours. When unexpected twists and turns arise, the two must save Metropolis together. Meanwhile, Lex Luthor has plans of his own and when he gets his hands on the serum that granted Lois superpowers, he becomes as powerful as Superman.

Can the Last Son of Krypton stop his arch nemesis while also saving the Earth from a damaged sun before he perishes?

When I think of classic Superman, I think of this story. The reason is because this story involves all of the classic elements of Superman lore, everything from the basics like Lois Lane and Lex Luthor, all the way to the Fortress of Solitude, the bottle city of Kandor, a full array of superpowers—and in the case of this story, some new ones, which reminds me of the "bonus" powers portrayed in *Superman IV* (though they're not silly in this one like they were in that flick)—the Phantom Zone, Superman using not only his super brawn but also his super brains, Lois having superpowers (which has happened quite a lot in Supes's history—she's got a cool costume in this, by the way), and a ton more.

Based on the graphic novel by Grant Morrison and Frank Quitely, this flick asks the hard questions about Superman's mortality, if such a thing is possible, and if it *is* possible, then how would that possibly play out? Unlike Superman's death when the Man of Steel went up against Doomsday, this story isn't about a giant slugfest, but about a slow death caused by the very thing that gives Superman his powers: the sun. It's about him coming to terms with his own mortality and setting things in order before his final moment arrives.

One of the great things about these direct-to-DVD super flicks from DC is they're all stand-alone features based on a graphic novel and by being so, they also carry with it the same art style from the book. In this case, it's Frank Quitely's art animated. I admit it took a while for his art to grow on me. Perhaps because it's so simple and clean, yet by being that way, he's able to create some pretty realistic-looking superheroes. Seeing it animated like we do in this flick brings Superman et al. to life and makes this comic book fan very happy.

Out of all the Superman adaptations done thus far, *All-Star Superman* is one of the greats and gets high props for being an awesome animated flick with a great cast, great art direction, a great story and, most importantly, having the greatest hero of them all, one who's definitely an all-star: Superman.

Highly recommended.

The Amazing Spider-Man (2012)
Written by James Vanderbilt, Alvin Sargent and Steve Kloves
Directed by Marc Webb
Runtime 136 min.
4 out of 5

After getting bitten by a genetically-modified spider, teenager Peter Parker discovers he has spider-like abilities. However, after looking into his past, he meets Dr. Conors and becomes the scientist's pupil. When Peter's uncle is murdered in cold blood, he uses his new spider abilities to try and track down the killer and ends up creating an alternate identity in the process. Meanwhile, Dr. Conors's own limb-regeneration experiments goes haywire and the good doctor is transformed into a giant lizard. Peter, now under the identity of Spider-Man, takes it upon himself to stop the Lizard at all costs before others get hurt.

When I first heard they were rebooting Spider-Man, I was like, "Come on, really? You just did that in the movies, the cartoons, in the comics . . ." It seems Spider-Man has only one story to tell: his origin. They keep doing it, after all.

But I got something more than that in *The Amazing Spider-Man* and I was won over. While I enjoyed the Raimi films on the whole, this one seemed more comic book Spider-Man to me as they dialed back the clock all the way to his childhood and got a bit more into Peter Parker's (Andrew Garfield's) parents' history, introduced Gwen Stacy (Emma Stone), and went with a villain that fans have been itching to see ever since his civilian identity was mentioned back in the 2002 *Spider-Man* movie: Dr. Conors aka the Lizard (Rhys Ifans). While Spidey's origin stayed true to its main components—getting bitten by a spider, Peter Parker as a student, the tragic death of Uncle Ben—they modernized it a bit and seemed to suggest that, kind of like in the 2003 *Hulk* movie, our hero's destiny was mapped out for him many years before. This part I wasn't too keen on, to be honest, nor was I big on how the Peter Parker side of things was done: pretty cool dude, likeable, good looking, hot girlfriend, etc. Pretty much the opposite of nerdy Parker becoming a superhero.

However, on the Spider-Man side of things, we got one wicked webcrawler on our hands. We've got three movies prior to this one to learn how to make him move, swing around, climb walls, spin webs—everything that was showcased in this flick was like a comic book come to life. What made it work, too, was that it was believable and didn't look like a 3D cartoon unlike some sequences in 2002's *Spider-Man*. What made it even more special was that this Spider-Man actually cracked a lot of jokes, something that was missing for the most part from the other outings. And the Spider-Man-point-of-view wall crawling and swinging around scenes? Yes, please! Totally made you feel like you were there and reminded me a lot of the Spider-Man ride at Universal Studios in Florida. Bring back the mechanical webshooters instead of the organic variety (I didn't mind those, actually, as it makes more sense), and Spider-Man is back in business, baby!

The stakes were high in this movie, too, with the Lizard being a serious bad guy to contend with. He was strong, powerful, showed no mercy, and that sewer scene was spooky.

This movie was a lay-the-groundwork movie, setting things up for what is currently rumored to be three sequels and, according to director Marc Webb, aiming for the Sinister Six storyline, which was being mapped out even while they were making this Spider-Man movie. I can't wait. A giant Spider-Man story is going to be awesome and I'm glad they started from scratch to make it happen as they can then link everything together, starting from scene one.

So what can I say? I've been pulled to the other side and am glad they rebooted Spider-Man. A part of me can't help but wonder what might've been had *Spider-Man 4* happened, but this new journey we're on with our favorite webhead is off to a good start.

The Avengers (2012)
Written by Joss Whedon
Directed by Joss Whedon
Runtime 143 min.
4 out of 5

When Thor's mischievous brother, Loki, makes a deal with the alien race the Chitauri to help them secure the Tesseract Cube so they can conquer the galaxy, the Earth suddenly falls into great peril. With even the powerful top secret agency S.H.I.E.L.D. having difficulty containing Loki, there is only one call S.H.I.E.L.D. Director Nick Fury can make: Avengers Assemble!

The team is gathered—Captain America, Iron Man, Thor, Hulk, Black Widow, Hawkeye—and they set out to do battle with Loki and his alien cohorts. If they don't overcome their differences and learn to work together as a team, the Earth will fall and Loki will rule the planet.

The Avengers brings together Earth's mightiest heroes to combat a force of evil so great they either stand together or fall together, with the fate of the planet—even the galaxy—hanging in the balance.

The Avengers is a difficult movie to review, more so, give a proper rating to because this movie is very much black and white between its story and its presentation, so that said, I'm going to quickly go over both and you'll see where I'm coming from at the end.

The story: This is a single-plot movie, very much an A-to-B narrative and incredibly simple—too simple. Aliens are coming, we need to stop them so we'll get the Avengers to do it. That's it. From a storytelling perspective, it's too simple and too predictable. Big bad guy, big good guy(s), let's fight, good guys win. The end.

However, if you view *The Avengers* as an end cap/final act to all the movies leading up to it: *Iron Man, Incredible Hulk, Iron Man 2, Thor, Captain America*—then you have something that definitely serves its purpose and more or less lets each character shine for the same amount of time. In this case, a simple story works despite, um, the many continuity flaws from the previous movies (i.e. Thor is somehow now able to come to Earth, which renders the ending of Thor's movie moot; Tony Stark called upon to be Iron Man in *The Avengers* despite being banned from doing so in *Iron Man 2*; the characters communicating to each other without earpieces or any communication devices. Maybe they're telepathic?).

The presentation: this movie is a nerd's dream come true from start to finish. Assemble your favorite superheroes—of which each were spotlighted in their own movies, almost—put them together and have them go toe-to-toe with a larger-than-life threat that will squash the planet if they don't come through.

From an eye candy perspective, this movie nailed it. Huge battles, lots of explosions, combat action, hammer throwing, Hulk smashing, shield boomeranging, repulsors firing, arrows shooting, girl fists punching—yeah, it has it all.

It's also very important to point out that the casting of Mark Ruffalo as Bruce Banner/Hulk was an amazing choice. I honestly wasn't too thrilled with the news when I first heard it, with Ruffalo being more of a chick-flick romance guy, but he got the role done so well that if there's a spin-off, I hope he gets the job. He's definitely earned it.

Chris Evans as Captain America—a Superman performance, which is good and brought a traditional superhero element to the team. As the running joke was throughout the movie, a little "old-fashioned" was what was needed.

Robert Downey Jr. as Iron Man—do I really need to talk about this? He's the same Tony Stark from the first two Iron Man movies, the only difference being he's mellowed out a bit because, despite his arrogance, he understands life isn't all about him and there are other people out there, too. This bit really comes through in this movie.

Chris Hemsworth as Thor—bold, poetic, commanding, everything his character is supposed to be so kudos to him for carrying on with a great performance from the stand-alone movie.

Jeremy Renner as Hawkeye—I don't know much about the comic character other than he's like Green Arrow, but perhaps with a more military-mind-set, so I can't comment. Renner did sell me on Hawkeye though, but why couldn't they give him that awesome mask? Maybe in the sequel.

Scarlett Johansson as Black Widow—she really comes into her own in this flick because in *Iron Man 2*, it was more a back-up appearance so we didn't know much about her. I'm glad she got the screen time she deserved and, come on, her fight scenes were fantastic.

Tom Hiddleston as Loki—he's the bad guy you love to hate, the one that, even just looking at him, you want to punch in the face. I appreciated how Loki, to a degree, was a villain to sympathize with because of his exile, but you also get mad at him for being such a jerk about it.

Samuel L. Jackson as Nick Fury—an excellent portrayal of Samuel L. Jackson being Samuel L. Jackson—but under a fictitious alias. Yeah.

The Avengers is a solid good-times-turn-your-brain-off-action-fest that is great for escape and is recommended for that reason. As a spoiler warning, if you want just the action parts, start the movie around thirty minutes in.

Honest assessment is 3.5 out of 5, but because it's the first movie of its kind and because of all the building up to it that has been going on since 2008, I'll give it a 4.

Batman (1966)
Written by Lorenzo Semple Jr.
Directed by Leslie H. Martinson
Runtime 105 min.
4 out of 5

Atomic batteries to power. Turbines to speed!

The dynamic duo, Batman and Robin, hit the big screen in this 1960s action/adventure camp-stravaganza!

When the caped crusaders's most dangerous foes—Joker, Riddler, Catwoman, Penguin—team up and plot to dehydrate the United Nations Security Council, Batman and Robin find themselves in over their heads and must pull out all the stops to put an end to the evil villains' dastardly plans in this big screen adaptation of the hit TV series.

This movie rocks! And here's why:

It's fast-paced, exciting, and is the definition of superhero fun. What? You mean superheroes can be fun? Of course! Remember dressing up as a kid and flying around the house as Superman or climbing the stairs as Spider-Man or swinging from room to room as Batman? Remember laying waste to all those imaginary villains while also saving the damsel in distress and trying to ignore your parents when they called you for dinner? *That* was superhero fun. Easy-going, super adventure.

This film is the same thing . . . but with grownups. Of course, it's also a giant *Batman* TV episode complete with such goodies as the animated THOKs and POWs bursting across the screen, crazy bat-gadgets for every occasion (i.e. the [in]famous bat-shark repellent), a host of bat-vehicles, and goofy special effects that work well in the context of the movie.

What's brilliant about this Batman movie are the jokes. First, it's meant to be silly and funny, but the humor is both overt and subtle, whether it's the dialogue, facial expressions or even actions in some cases. It's also amazing that despite it being purposely campy, Adam West and Burt Ward—Batman and Robin, respectively—played their characters straight. What I mean is, they played these guys seriously in the crazy, colorful world they inhabited—the characters matching the story, the environment and those they interacted with—and not once did it seem like actors goofing around and simply scoring a paycheck. That's a feat on its own, in my books.

Nowadays, superhero filmmakers have a hard time trying to do more than one villain in their movies. Why they don't go back and look at this flick for help, I don't know. Granted, the four villains in here all had their TV history backing them up, but they still were able to each stand on their own and each share the spotlight and fulfill their roles. No one is second stringer to anyone else.

If there is a movie out there that represents superhero fantasy, this flick is it. Everything is so over-the-top that it actually works and you feel like you're watching an old school comic book come to life. Joel Schumacher tried to recreate this with *Batman Forever* and *Batman & Robin* and wasn't able to pull it off. The big reason, in my mind, is because he tried to merge the old with the new and that's like mixing black and white—you get a bunch of gray and no one knows what's what.

Anyway, I love this movie. My kids love this movie and I let them watch it because compared to the ultra dark Bat-flicks of today, I need to know they'll have fun watching a Bat-movie, will have at least a general sense of what's going on, and won't get nightmares after. (I mean, Heath Ledger's Joker creeps me out and I'm an adult.)

Batman is one of my all-time favorite movies. It's lighthearted, it's funny, it's exciting, and is a showcase of everything that made the TV series such a hit, even now, nearly fifty years later.

Recommended.

Batman (1989)
Written by Sam Hamm and Warren Skaaren
Directed by Tim Burton
Runtime 126 min.
4 out of 5

There are rumors of a six-foot bat in Gotham City. Whispers. Suggestions. Nothing concrete. But all that changes after the Batman confronts Carl Grissom's men at Axis Chemicals and Grissom's top hood, Jack Napier, gets dropped into a vat of chemicals, transforming him into the maniacal Joker. Discovering he had been set up by his boss to take the fall at Axis, Joker takes over Grissom's operation, in turn allowing him to try and take over Gotham City itself, with only the Dark Knight to stop him.

This was the film that gave us the "movie Batman" we know today: dark and armored. If it wasn't for director Tim Burton's gothic and grim vision of crime-ridden Gotham City and its brooding protector, I suspect the edgy superhero movies of today wouldn't exist.

Michael Keaton takes on the title role as billionaire playboy Bruce Wayne and his rubber-clad alter ego Batman, delivering one of the greatest Batman performances that many, at the time, hadn't expected from "Mr. Mom." And after his memorable line during the opening rooftop scene, "I'm Batman," from that moment on he had you sold that his version of the Dark Knight meant business and quenches any lingering thought that Batman, thanks to the 1960s TV series, is a campy superhero.

Stealing the stage is Jack Nicholson as the Joker. Basically take the Jack from *One Flew Over the Cuckoo's Nest* and crank it up to a hundred and you have the Joker. Nicholson does a brilliant job of blending the serious and twisted Joker while also playing the crazy, laughing, psycho killer. I'm sure when *Batman: The Animated Series* came along, Nicholson's Joker was the template for Mark Hamill's performance when he voiced the character. Awesome.

Danny Elfman's haunting and lonely score only adds to the movie's eeriness.

My only problem with the film was there wasn't enough Batman. I remember that bothering me as a kid. Batman shows up all of four times in the film, the first being something, like, only for a minute. Each subsequent time gets progressively longer, thankfully.

Bold, atmospheric and downright fun, *Batman* is one for the ages. It was where the modern dark superhero movie started.

Batman & Robin (1997)
Written by Akiva Goldsman
Directed by Joel Schumacher
Runtime 125 min.
2 out of 5

A freeze is coming.

Gotham is under siege, this time by not one but *three* supervillains: Mr. Freeze (Arnold Schwarzenegger), Poison Ivy (Uma Thurman) and Bane (Jeep Swenson).

The Dynamic Duo (George Clooney and Chris O'Donnell) is called to the rescue despite the tension growing between them. Complicating things, Barbara Pennyworth (Alicia Silverstone), Alfred's niece, has come to Wayne Manor to liberate her ailing uncle from a life of servitude. She also has a secret: a wild side that needs to be tamed.

When an all-out assault is declared on Gotham by Mr. Freeze and Poison Ivy, the caped crusaders rise to the occasion, and this time they have a little help.

If you took the cheesy, camp-filled '60's *Batman* series and shot it with a huge budget, tons of effects and modern day equipment, *Batman & Robin* is what you'd get (and is what we got).

Clearly this was the film that killed the Batman franchise. It took eight years for Warner Brothers to recover from the disaster that was this movie.

The story—the "what it's about"—though farfetched, is bearable. It's the dialogue and stupid jokes that catapult this Bat-flick a zillion miles into the campy canyon.

On the plus side, if you watch this movie solely for the bright colors, glitter and action, you'll have a good time.

If you're looking for substance, go back to the beginning, namely Burton's '89 triumph.

Batman and Mr. Freeze: SubZero (1998)
Written by Boyd Kirkland and Randy Rogel
Directed by Boyd Kirkland
Runtime 70 min.
4 out of 5

In an effort to save his dying wife, Nora, Victor Fries (aka Mr. Freeze) kidnaps Barbara Gordon, Commissioner Gordon's daughter because his wife needs an organ transplant and Barbara possesses the same rare blood type as his ailing wife. Batman and Robin are quickly hot on his tail and soon it's a game of cat and mouse between the Dynamic Duo and Mr. Freeze as our heroes seek to find Barbara before it's too late and she falls victim to Mr. Freeze's evil plan.

After the amazing thrill that was *Batman: Mask of the Phantasm*, and when I heard they were making another Batman animated movie, I was pumped. *Mask of the Phantasm* was insanely good and since *SubZero* was to be done in the same style by the same people, my expectations were high. While not as good as *Phantasm*, *SubZero* is still a solid flick. What makes it cool is it's a team-up movie because Batman's joined by Robin, something *Phantasm* didn't have. You also get to briefly see Batgirl in costume in this one as well.

Mr. Freeze is a tricky bad guy because while powerful, you take away his freeze gun and he's got nothing and it's easy to turn him into a one-trick-pony that way and diminish the complicated character that he is. Not in *SubZero*. You get to see Mr. Freeze for who he is under that armor and, well, he's just a heartbroken guy who's doing what he believes is the right thing. So distraught over his wife's fatal illness but brilliant enough to figure out a cure, he's willing to stop at nothing to save the woman he loves, even if that means killing an innocent person in the process. For those who have gone through immense heartbreak, you know how easy it is for unclear thinking to reign and how nothing but emotion takes over.

This flick also showed how Batman and Robin feed off each other and work together, and not in that "Way to go, chum" way that was the staple of the 1960s *Batman* series. You see two professional crime fighters playing off each other's strengths, giving each other ideas, each keeping the other encouraged and balanced as they fight the good fight.

There was also some 3D animation in this movie, back when 3D was a new thing. While the 3D parts didn't blend against the 2D as seamlessly as they do nowadays, it did add a "wow" factor to the flick—for its time—and kept Batman on the cutting edge of animation.

I'm really pleased with this movie and it gets better with each viewing, and with an ending that is both sad but satisfying, *Batman and Mr. Freeze: SubZero* is a Bat-movie that should be part of any Bat-fan's collection.

Batman Begins *(2005)*
Written by Christopher Nolan and David S. Goyer
Directed by Christopher Nolan
Runtime 140 min.
5 out of 5

Bruce Wayne's parents are brutally murdered right before his eyes. He is only eight years old. His father holds his hand. His mother lays in her own blood beside them. His father's dying words: "Don't be afraid."

Vowing vengeance, Bruce travels the world, learning all that he can to become a one-man army against crime. He leaves behind the life of a billionaire playboy and instead seeks to find the man rooted in pain and anger, the one inside him.

Trained by a man named Ducard, a representative of Ra's Al Ghul, Bruce learns how to harness his rage and use it to exact vengeance on those who would dare break the law.

But to do so as Bruce Wayne would only put those he cares about in danger and would not be the symbol required to get the job done, and so is born . . . the Batman.

Drugs are secretly being pumped into Gotham City's waterways, the underground crime circuit somehow connected to a mysterious figure overseas who has big plans for Gotham. No one knows his face . . . until it's too late.

Jonathan Crane, aka the Scarecrow, uses his position in Arkham Asylum to get the inmates gathered for what's to come, and when the moment finally arrives, all hell breaks loose on Gotham's streets.

The night grows dim, the knight grows dark.

Batman is born.

Wowser.

This flick was amazing.

After the disaster that was *Batman & Robin*, I was so scared about how this would turn out. Sure, the trailers looked cool, dark, and edgy, but studios always put the best bits in the trailers anyway. All we had were hopes and good-sounding quotes from those involved in the film's production.

And, man, did they deliver!

This stuff was real. Real-real. *Batman Begins* was grounded in reality in a way I hadn't seen since *X-men*. This stuff could really happen. It was that tone that brought a level of seriousness to the movie that the other Bat-flicks—except *Batman* in 1989—didn't have. This wasn't a superhero movie, but a story about a man lost in rage, darkness and needing a way out. It was about the very real contrast between revenge and justice, and making right what once went so terribly wrong.

It's a story about redemption, love, and fighting to protect strangers in a city where crime, filth and evil are the everyday norm.

Christian Bale *is* Batman. Period. When the mask was on, you could tell Bruce was channeling pure rage and distaste for evil, focusing all that anger on the task before him. When the mask was off, he was the Bruce Wayne who was a spoiled rich boy, dumb, and no one took seriously. Excellent duality.

Katie Holmes as Bruce's childhood friend/love interest, Rachel Dawes, was a good thing. The other Bat-movies always had a girlfriend for him. Though there was romantic interest here, it was rooted in friendship, which was a nice change.

Michael Caine as Alfred—brilliant. He was your loving father-figure, yet was stern with Bruce when the need arose, and even got behind him despite reservation when Bruce told him his grand plan for saving Gotham. Only the love of a friend would allow such a thing: to believe in an ideal and not necessarily the method.

Cillian Murphy was downright creepy as Jonathan Crane/Scarecrow. I only knew him from *28 Days Later* so wasn't sure how he'd play this. Let's just say I was happy.

Liam Neeson as Ducard/Ra's Al Ghul was all right. As Ducard, sure, made sense. He did a great job as Bruce's mentor. The two were the same at heart. Just chose different paths. As Ra's—that twist didn't surprise me (solely because I stumbled upon the script online before I saw the actual movie), but it did surprise me in the sense that Liam Neeson will always be Qui-Gon Jinn to me. It was hard to see him as a bad guy.

Gary Oldman *is* James Gordon. He looked the part, acted the part, and I fully sympathized with him being pretty much the only good cop in a bad town.

Batman Begins is the quintessential Bat-film.

Very recommended. Ten times over.

Batman Beyond: Return of the Joker (2000)
Written by Paul Dini
Directed by Curt Geda
Runtime 77 min.
5 out of 5

He was thought dead. The laughter was supposed to have ended.
But evil never dies.
The Joker is back!
His mission? Why, give Gotham a wedgy again!
But this Gotham is different than the one the Joker left behind. It's a new Gotham with a new Batman.
Plenty of surprises abound in this thrilling chapter in the *Batman Beyond* universe.

This movie is brilliant, pure and simple.
I've seen both the regular and the uncut versions of this film and it's the uncut version that's being reviewed here (the regular is virtually the same and has only a few altered scenes).
The uncut version doesn't hold back and isn't sensitive to the viewer's eyes. This one's much more violent than the regular version. In the original release, certain events were only implied. In this one, they are shown. (If anything, I was surprised at how graphic this cartoon was compared to the *Batman Beyond* and *Batman: TAS* episodes.)
Ah, yes, the joys of direct-to-DVD releases.
The Batman in *Batman Beyond*, Terry McGinnis, is real. You care about him, you relate to him. You want to be him even when the tension mounts between him and his mentor, Bruce Wayne.
The Joker's nasty in this and once more Mark Hamill, with that creepy laugh of his, reminds us why he was born to play the Joker. The dialogue, the jokes—utterly fantastic!
The story is stellar, with multiple plots going on at once. It also answers the questions you have about the fate of the characters from *Batman: TAS*, which had a series finale that fell flat. (It was just another episode, really.)
The first time I saw this film I couldn't believe what happened to one of the Bat regulars. It still blows me away every time I see it. Wow.

Batman Forever (1995)
Written by Lee Batchler, Janet Scott-Batchler and Akiva Goldsman
Directed by Joel Schumacher
Runtime 121 min.
3 out of 5

Two Face has been terrorizing Gotham for a while and after executing a terrible sentence at Gotham Circus, he inadvertently changes the life of the Dark Knight forever by setting in motion a chain of events that lead to the birth of Batman's legendary partner, Robin.

Continuing in the "double villain" trend as established by *Batman Returns*, a disgruntled—and stalker-ish—employee of Wayne Industries, Edward Nigma, gets revenge on his boss by becoming the Riddler, and steals his way to the top of the technology enterprise game.

It's two-on-two in this third installment of the Batman franchise.

Riddle me this: what do you get when you cross Adam West and Michael Keaton? You get Val Kilmer's portrayal of Batman, one who is part serious and part humorous. This is the film that I've always viewed as the "transition piece" between the dark Bat-flicks done by Tim Burton and the all-out camp-fest that is *Batman & Robin*.

Though a bit over the top, the story of *Batman Forever* is a good one and if you watch it just for that, you'll highly enjoy it.

It was the humor that brought this film down.

First, Batman ain't funny. He's so serious and dry he makes Al Gore look like Superman.

Second, Two Face isn't funny. Tommy Lee Jones, as much as I enjoy him as an actor, got the character wrong. Two Face is a gangster not another version of the Joker.

Third, Riddler isn't all whacky and zany, though by director Joel Schumacher's choice to cast Jim Carrey in the role, it's evident he was after Frank Gorshin's Riddler from the '60s instead of the comic book Riddler. Jim also got this part shortly after he became super famous so obviously this role was playing to his strength of being a rubber-faced whack job.

Fourth, though it was a neat thing to add Robin to the mix, Chris O'Donnell was too old, but, I suppose, having a kid running around in an anatomically-correct rubber suit would have raised too many questions.

This film was 50/50 for me. Had its pluses and minuses. I'm going to leave this in the "decide for yourself" category.

Batman: Gotham Knight (2008)

Written by Brian Azzarello, Josh Olson, David S. Goyer, Greg Rucka, Jordan Goldberg and Alan Burnett

Directed by Yasuhiro Aoki, Yuichiro Hayashi, Futoshi Higashide, Toshiyuki Kubooka, Hiroshi Morioka, Jong-Sik Nam and Shojiro Nishimi

Runtime 75 min.

4.5 out of 5

Okay, now this is how you do something new with a character and do it right and totally change the formula. Not only was the style of Batman animation changed—this whole movie is done in anime by genuine Japanese anime directors—but also instead of giving us one big story, why not give us six shorter ones in the same universe?

This flick was meant as a bridge between *Batman Begins* and *The Dark Knight*, giving audiences an in-depth glimpse into Batman's past and what he's been up to between those two movies. To make it even sweeter, Kevin Conroy voices Batman for all six short films.

They are (and what I thought):

Have I Got a Story for You -

Premise: A bunch of skater kids relate to each other firsthand encounters with the Dark Knight.

Really good, each story seeming to center around Batman chasing the same thief. The art direction is ridiculous! Did you see the backgrounds in this thing? While the character designs for this vignette were so-so, the backgrounds were insane. What makes this vignette special is it shows how the Batman legend was born, that is, people swapping stories, relating what they thought they saw versus what really happened, and how one tale leads to another until, eventually, Batman is myth and man combined.

Of course, sometimes the facts get straightened out, as per the ending of this story. You'll have to see for yourself what I mean.

Crossfire -

Premise: Two cops take a recently-dropped-off-by-Batman felon to the Narrows for incarceration. There they encounter tons of trouble and Batman comes to the rescue.

This one is much grittier than the previous story, focusing heavily on the cops and gangs. The art is superb and while the backgrounds are more classical animation, the character design is top notch and I really dig how everyone looks in this tale. Batman is boss in this: big, powerful, sleek, tough—wish he looked like this all the time. Well done.

The main point of the story is the question: is Batman an ally? One cop thinks so, the other is skeptical, and the conclusion reached? Well, you'll just have to see this wicked cartoon for yourself.

Field Test -

Premise: Lucius Fox shows Bruce Wayne some new gear he can use as Batman and he gets a chance to do just that.

How does anyone draw this good? The backgrounds are so realistic it's upsetting (in that good way). The character design is very classic anime: pointier noses, smaller eyes, very realistic body proportions.

Batman definitely has a unique style to his suit in this; not your classic uniform but it works. I also like the change of pace by showing his eyes instead of having just whites. I think this is the first time Batman's been animated that way.

All in all, this vignette was great and there is a moral to the story about Batman's stance on guns and how he understands the need to defend himself against them . . . but not at another's expense.

In Darkness Dwells -

Premise: When a congregation starts going crazy during a church service, Batman thinks the Scarecrow is to blame. Instead, he's greeted by someone far more dangerous: Killer Croc! However, Scarecrow is still waiting in the wings.

Visually, this vignette is very comic-book-like. I see glimpses of Mike Mignola's—*Hellboy* artist and creator—style though I doubt that the animators were trying to imitate that. It's just what it reminds me of.

This one was pretty exciting. Lots of action, lots of danger, lots of Batman stopping baddies and getting out of tight situations. Dig it.

LOOK, UP ON THE SCREEN!

Working Through Pain -

Premise: Suffering from a gunshot wound, Batman flashes back to before he donned the cowl and reflects on pain and what it means in his life physically and emotionally.

This one's pretty gory, but that's to further cement the point of this tale: pain . . . and what it does for Batman, how he deals with it and how he overcomes it. Giving glimpses into Bruce Wayne's travels and the training he picked up along the way, we get to see the lengths he went to to perfect his body in the areas of enduring through pain—physical and emotional—something he no doubt knew he needed to do if he was to succeed in his mission. Except, there is one pain he can't overcome.

Visually, I liked the art style of this one as well.

Deadshot -

Premise: Deadshot comes to Gotham and the word is he's going to assassinate Jim Gordon. When the GCPD catch wind of this, they let Batman know. Batman becomes Gordon's shadow and resolves to keep his friend safe.

The art direction in this is like a high-end comic book come to life. Really, really liked it. Great line work, crisp images, solid colors, dark and bleak like a Batman comic. Awesome. And that train tunnel? Gotta be a 3D background but it looks unbelievably cool.

The Batman-vs-Deadshot battle is a sweet one, high speed on a train.

The main thrust of this story is about guns and how Batman feels about them. Since it was a gun that killed his parents, it's a touchy area for him.

All six of these stories were well done, well thought out and well written. I'm proud to be a Batman fan while watching these and I'm equally happy DC tried something new with the character and succeeded in spades. By tying this animated flick into the live action ones, it added a whole new dimension to those stories and to these animated shorts as well.

Long live Batman!

Batman: Mask of the Phantasm (1993)
Written by Alan Burnett, Paul Dini, Martin Pasko and Michael Reaves
Directed by Eric Radomski and Bruce Timm
Runtime 76 min.
5 out of 5

A mysterious costumed phantasm haunts Gotham City, knocking off mob bosses thus drawing the Batman out from the shadows to stop him. Only when the Dark Knight starts to uncover clues as to who this person might be does he discover how deeply personal this phantasm's crusade has become, not just to the phantasm himself, but to the Batman as well.

Pulling out all the stops with top-notch storytelling, animation and direction, *Batman: Mask of the Phantasm* is a hallmark in Batman's movie history that's guaranteed not to disappoint!

This movie is unbelievably amazing and rivals even the almighty *Dark Knight Trilogy* that would begin on the big screen twelve years later. Actually, *Mask of the Phantasm* was in theatres and I remember going there with a friend and being stunned start to finish at this masterpiece. I also remember being anxious for it to hit home video—and back then, flicks took a looong time to get to video—and the day it came out, I went to K-Mart straight after school, spent some big bucks for the VHS (over twenty, I'm sure), then biked home in the rain so I could watch it. It was totally worth that brutal and soaked-to-the-bone bike ride.

This is a serious Bat-flick, both in tone and scope. Brought to life by the same team that managed *Batman: The Animated Series*—Bruce Timm and Paul Dini—I'm pretty sure this was the first animated superhero movie to ever hit the big screen. This was also at a time when animated superhero movies never happened. There were only half-hour shows— twenty-two minutes, technically—and that was it.

The story is enthralling, right from the introduction of the mysterious phantasm through Bruce Wayne's heartbreaking journey both in the present day and in the flashbacks that showcased his rise as the Dark Knight, all the way to the intense, sobering and heart-wrenching finish.

To this day, *Mask of the Phantasm* stands as a benchmark of Batman storytelling in my book. It's right up there with the *Dark Knight Trilogy,*

Batman 1989, and the other recent animated efforts. Personally, it's the finest superhero animated effort ever brought to screen.

The storyline is mature and, probably due to it hitting theatres, was geared toward adults as it clearly contained those kinds of markings (i.e. a hinted-at sex scene between Bruce and Andrea, something that was never in superhero animation before). The violence level was also a notch above the animated series, complete with blood, hard-hitting brutality, and a glimpse into the kinds of real-life physical ordeals Batman would have to go through if he truly existed.

The real strength of the story lies in the fact that as much as it's Batman solving a mystery, it's Bruce Wayne's story, showing us a part of his journey to becoming Batman, what made him finally put on the cape and cowl, and how those events from his past had a direct and painful impact not just on his future, but on the future of Gotham City as well.

The animation is perfect, moody, stylized and has become the benchmark even all these years later of what superhero animation can be.

This isn't a kids movie. This is a serious Bat-movie for the serious Bat-fan who wants to take their Bat-flick experience to the next level.

Highly recommended.

Batman: Mystery of the Batwoman (2003)
Written by Michael Reaves
Directed by Curt Geda
Runtime 75 min.
5 out of 5

There's a new superhero in Gotham, one who wears silver-gray tights and a cape.

And she's a woman, a *bat*-woman.

At first it appears she's here to help, but when she begins targeting the Penguin and Rupert Thorne's secret arms operation, the Dark Knight and the Boy Wonder step in to solve the mystery of the Batwoman.

Who is she? What does she want? And why is it each time Batman thinks he's solved her secret identity does he find himself back at square one?

As Batman and Batwoman put the strain on the Penguin's operation, the bird man calls in a deadly force to eliminate them: Bane.

The Bruce Timm-designed Batman series is a staple on the animated superhero genre. The sleek yet angler style's been used in *Batman: The Animated Series*, *Batman Beyond*, *Superman: The Animated Series*, *Justice League* and *Justice League Unlimited*. And in *Batman: Mystery of the Batwoman*, it's delivered in spades. The art is just simply amazing straight through.

The story is terrific, with twists and turns right up 'til the end, and no punches are pulled in giving each and every character a level of depth not usually achieved in animated features.

Kevin Conroy *is* Batman and has the greatest Batman voice out of them all, both live action and animated. His line delivery as the Dark Knight forces you to respect the pointy-eared vigilante and take him seriously. The dude's got major authority.

Likewise, Efrem Zimbalist Jr. as Alfred? Wow. Between him and Kevin, these two hold down the film and set the tone for the entire movie. The relationship Alfred and Bruce Wayne share is beyond close and is a stark contrast to the relationships the bat-women suspects have with their own family or loved ones.

You know what? All the voices were terrific, not a one out of place. Each suited the character they portrayed, the acting and tone behind their voices never missing a beat.

The stakes are high, the danger's real and Batman is better than ever. Go. Watch. Enjoy.

Batman Returns (1992)
Written by Daniel Waters
Directed by Tim Burton
Runtime 126 min.
3.5 out of 5

A mysterious "penguin man" surfaces and takes the city by storm, so much so that evil business tycoon Max Shreck, played by Christopher Walken, thinks he can turn Penguin into the city's new mayor. But Penguin is not all what he seems and he secretly controls the Red Triangle Gang, who are wreaking havoc across the city.

Adding to the mix is one Selina Kyle, Shreck's lowly assistant, er, secretary, who, after a bad night with her boss, becomes Catwoman.

The Bat Signal shines and the Dark Knight returns to once again rid Gotham of chaos and restore order.

Michael Keaton is back as Gotham's Guardian and brings to the role all the mystery and edge that made the '89 movie so popular. What's even better is that this movie actually has Batman in it and the vigilante appears, clad in black armor, more than just four times like in the previous flick.

Danny DeVito as the Penguin does a great job given what he had to work with. Though the Penguin in this film is not the same as the one in the comics, DeVito still did well portraying a man who was born . . . a little different.

Michelle Pfeiffer pulls off the dual role of Selina Kyle/Catwoman nicely. In fact, she plays four distinct roles in this film, all in one character: nerdy Selina, hip Selina, crazy Selina and Catwoman.

This film is filled with action, darkness and fun, all set in Tim Burton's eerie Gotham City, which was a character on its own in this film and its predecessor.

It's the hokey plot that's earning this film a lower rating than the previous one. Had the story been better, this movie had the potential to be one of the best superhero flicks ever.

The Batman vs Dracula (2005)
Written by Duane Capizzi
Directed by Michael Goguen
Runtime 83 min.
4 out of 5

What starts as a treasure hunt by the Penguin soon turns into a near-apocalyptic ordeal when he accidentally revives the legendary Dracula. Immediately, the prince of darkness begins to feed, snatching innocent citizens of Gotham from its streets.

Darkness blankets the city and the Caped Crusader is all who stands in the way between Dracula and the city's doom.

Wow. That was my first reaction when watching this. This direct-to-DVD release doesn't view as your standard Batman cartoon. This truly is a monster tale and views more like a horror movie than a superhero flick.

The vampires in this film are scary, looking like something between a vampire and a zombie. Dracula himself is neat, trim and suave, yet carries a presence of death.

This DVD also introduces Batman's love interest, Vicky Vale (who appeared both in the comics and in the 1989 movie). I have yet to discover how much of a role she will have in the half-hour episodes of *The Batman* series (I have only watched up to season three), but it was great to see her on screen. It was also wonderful to see Bruce Wayne dealing with a female lead in a realistic way and having once again come face-to-face with Batman getting in the way of his personal life.

A surprising touch to this film was the Joker, not so much the character but what happens to him. Cool indeed.

This is a solid Bat-flick, one which is definitely meant for an older audience, not for kids. Thirteen or fourteen and up, I'd say.

This flick is a keeper, one every true Bat-fan should have.

Batman: Year One (2011)
Written by Tab Murphy
Directed by Sam Liu and Lauren Montgomery
Runtime 64 min.
4.5 out of 5

After spending many years abroad, Bruce Wayne returns to Gotham City to fulfill the vow to rid it of crime that he made to his deceased parents when he was a boy. At the same time, Chicago cop James Gordon moves to Gotham to start with the GCPD. Soon, Bruce adopts the identity of the Batman and makes war on Gotham's crime families, with James Gordon hot on his tail as the cop tries to take down the vigilante crime fighter.

I love origin stories. The mythology of characters, their history, their motivations, the events leading up to the creation of a super identity—all of it's gold in my book. *Batman: Year One* is such a story, giving you not only Batman's origin, but the chance to walk a mile in his shoes during his first year as a crime fighter. You get to see him test the waters, make mistakes, have some wins and losses, and watch as he earns the trust of Gotham's finest.

This movie is a down-to-earth story about Batman and James Gordon, very much a crime story versus a superhero-vs-supervillain tale. Batman deals with real world criminals in real world ways. You also get a glimpse into the hard life he leads, what he gives up to be Batman, and how he balances life as a fool in the public eye so he could be a fear to the criminal underworld at night.

You also get to see a different side of James Gordon, the marriage trouble, his humanity, and the plight of being a good cop in a bad town. His portrayal makes him every bit a hero as Batman in this story.

This flick is based on the one-shot comic book by comics superstar Frank Millar and matches the book's style for the most part, really bringing it to life.

This is a story of beginnings so the pacing is different than what most people are used to, and instead of having a beginning, middle, big lead up to a climax then end, it has—to me, anyway—more of a beginning, middle and then part of an end because it's really a prequel to all the other Batman stories that come after it. Which is fine. It works, but I remember going, "Is that it?" when it ended after I first watched it.

I'm glad that Batman's first year was brought to the small screen and I hope more first year stories are made for other heroes. Superman next would be great.

Recommended.

Blade (1998)
Written by David S. Goyer
Directed by Stephen Norrington
Runtime 120 min.
4 out of 5

Half-human/half-vampire Blade makes war on the undead—that's the vampire undead, I'm talking—and tries to dismantle the vampire underworld piece by piece. He soon meets Karen, a hematologist, who was bitten by a vampire. Before the change occurs, she researches how a possible cure can be attained. Meanwhile, Deacon Frost, a rising star in the vampire community, believes he can become even more powerful by awakening the blood god La Magra. The problem is he needs the blood of the "daywalker"—Blade—to achieve it.

Blood and carnage ensue as Blade tries to stop the vampire world from rising to supremacy while also battling the bloodthirsty vampire within himself in this thrilling monster superhero movie extravaganza.

For me, *Blade* was the "prequel" movie to the start of the superhero box office comeback, which would later be kicked off by *X-Men*. It was almost as if studios were testing the waters with a serious superhero movie using a lesser known character and disguising him as a "slayer" to see how audiences would react. That's my superficial first impression, but then when you get into *Blade* and watch it you soon find out there is far more here than just a slayer-vs-vampire flick. Is he a superhero? Yes, but not your conventional one. There is no secret identity, no costume per se—though he does sport a cool trench coat and sword—and no standard supporting character in the vein of a love interest. Instead, you get a conflicted man who's part vampire who's trying so desperately to tame the beast within while also doing what's right: killing vampires and helping those who get caught in the crossfire. Sounds like a superhero to me.

Wesley Snipes as Blade is sheer awesomeness. He's tough as nails, got the martial arts moves, is dark and handles himself like someone who has the weight of the world on his shoulders. Which is true, of course, as he's doing his best to keep the vampires at bay, namely the ambitious ones who would seek to subdue, even eradicate, the human race.

Kris Kristofferson is dynamite as Whistler, Blade's father-figure, friend and mentor. Talk about a tragic origin for this guy and one that tugs at the heartstrings. He's the perfect example of a man trying to make things right because something so wrong was done to him and those he loved. Plus "Kris Kristofferson" is a cool name so he gets points just for that.

I liked Stephen Dorff as Deacon Frost, a cocky villain who knows how powerful he is and is tired of others trying to "keep a good vampire down." He'd make an amazing Bat-villain, in my mind, just by the way he plays villains—confident, dark, a tad witty—maybe Riddler? I mean, the real Riddler, the one who's serious and not a slapstick goofball like in *Batman Forever.*

Blade's exciting from start to finish, with action sequences and slayer-vs-vampire moments that make you want to hit the rewind on the remote and watch 'em again. I'm really glad they made two other sequels because Blade's a character with endless story possibilities because both him and his universe go beyond the simple slayer-vs-vampire motif. Like a Transformer, there's more to him than meets the eye and this flick does a great job of showing that. No wonder it did so well at the box office and earned about triple its budget.

Recommended.

Blade II (2002)
Written by David S. Goyer
Directed by Guillermo del Toro
Runtime 117 min.
4 out of 5

A major virus is sweeping the through the vampire community and transforming its hosts into creatures called Reapers, who have a thirst for blood worse than vampires, are near invulnerable, and who can also pass the virus on to victims of their own. Worse, they feed on both human and vampire alike. Desperate to stop these creatures, the vampire community strikes a truce with Blade and gets him to help them fight these awful creatures. As Blade carves his way through the Reapers, he finds out their sinister origin and must put a stop to the Reaper vampires once and for all.

The thing with sequels is you gotta go bigger and better than the first one. It's not always easy and usually fails, however there are exceptions and *Blade II* is such an exception. Instead of just simply pitting Blade against more vampires, he now has to fight alongside them and stop a common enemy. How does that go? "The enemy of my enemy is my friend"? That's what's happening here and is a unique take on the vampire mythos and takes Blade to the next level.

Wesley Snipes is back as the Daywalker, and does everything right in this flick like he did in the first movie: tough, sweet action, martial arts, swordplay, solid acting and more. It's always great when you can see the actor enjoys what they're doing—or convinces you they are—instead of merely phoning it in as is sometimes the case when an actor keeps reprising a role.

Kris Kristofferson is back, too, which is awesome because Whistler is a big part of the first movie and this one might've felt hollow without him. How they bring him back after what happened in the last movie was also clever.

The Reapers—total killers with sweet SFX, brutal savagery and they make the regular vampires look like a bunch of modern day angsty vamps by comparison. Always a good thing when you up the ante on the bad guy.

LOOK, UP ON THE SCREEN!

I really liked this sequel, especially because, like I said, it had a fresh take on the slayer-vs-vampire mythos and I'm all about fresh takes. The story moved along at a good clip, kept me engaged, and makes me have a good time every time I have a *Blade* movie marathon.

Awesome stuff, *Blade II*.

Recommended like the first.

Blade: Trinity (2004)
Written by David S. Goyer
Directed by David S. Goyer
Runtime 113 min.
3.5 out of 5

Things come to a head in this thrilling final chapter in the *Blade Trilogy*, pitting Blade against Drake aka Dracula, the king daddy of all vampires. Teaming up with Hannibal King and Abigail Whistler, the trio seeks to take down Dracula before he can create more daywalkers and eliminate Blade forever.

If you're going to bring things to a head and have a final showdown between the good guy and a major bad guy, you need to ensure that your major bad guy is a big deal and you don't really get any more big deal than Dracula. Created by Bram Stoker and based on the historical and infamous Vlad the Impaler, Dracula was the first vampire ever and has since become not only the most famous one, but has tons of media under his namesake including movies, books, TV shows, cartoons, songs—everything. And that's just him never mind the countless media sporting all the vampires he inspired. Taking a vampire hunter like Blade and putting him up against Dracula makes good sense to me.

Except the Dracula in this movie is pretty so-so, which doesn't cut it, in my opinion. I was expecting an ultra-powerful vampire, one that would give even the Reapers in *Blade II* a run for their money in terms of villain awesomeness. Instead, I was given a strong vampire, but not the ultimate vampire. Too bad, too, because having him as a bad guy is an awesome idea.

As always, Wesley Snipes leads the flick as the titular hero, picking up right where he left off in *Blade II* and staying consistent in character start to finish.

Having Ryan Reynolds as Hannibal King—I'm a Reynolds fan. Put him in the right role and you're guaranteed something good. Not sure how he stacks up against his comic book counterpart, but for this flick, not only was he tough as all get out and kicked all sorts of butt, but the comedic elements he brought had me laughing out loud more than once and yet such jokes worked in this movie and didn't seem out of place.

Jessica Biel as Abigail Whistler—who doesn't like a strong woman who can hold her own and fight vampires? I appreciated the seriousness she brought to the role and was a nice counterbalance to Hannibal King.

Kris Kristofferson was briefly back as Whistler, Abigail's father. Won't say more as I don't want to spoil anything for those who haven't seen the flick yet.

This movie has solid action throughout, but I wish the climactic battle between Dracula and Blade was more epic. Seemed average, but that could just be me. Really liked this movie on the whole, though. It was the Dracula angle that brought it down a notch solely because there was more they could've done in terms of raising the stakes with such a villain.

In the end, it's a decent send-off for Blade and a pretty good bookend to the trilogy.

Go check it out.

Blankman (1994)
Written by Damon Wayans and J.F. Lawton
Directed by Mike Binder
Runtime 92 min.
4 out of 5

Two brothers. One a nerd. One a Karate expert. Both grown up and living with their grandma.

Darryl and Kevin Walker (Damon Wayons and David Alan Grier) have lived in the rough part of town with their grandma since they were kids. As boys they'd run around the apartment with towels tied around their necks, aping Batman and Robin. Now, grown up, Kevin works at the TV station doing over-the-top news stories about aliens while Darryl works as a repairman and has a knack for inventing. After their grandma is killed along with several others while working to support the campaign of a wholesome, upcoming mayor, Darryl vows to make a difference in his city and invents bulletproof long johns, transforming himself into Blankman. He even makes a costume for his brother . . . who quickly refuses to join him. Taking cues from the campy 1960s *Batman* series, Blankman sets out to help others and uses this super alter ego to work through his grandmother's death. Meanwhile, Kevin lets Darryl go about his crimefighting business since he's too busy trying to woo beautiful reporter Kimberly Jonz (Robin Givens), who does *real* news stories several floors above him. Of course, tensions rise as Kimberly seems to have a thing for Blankman and admires the superhero's heroic efforts.

Eventually, Kevin learns who was behind their grandmother's death: the city's crime boss, Michael Minelli (Jon Polito). This time, Kevin asks to join Darryl on his crusade and since Darryl is the ever-faithful brother, he produces the outfit Kevin rejected and Kevin becomes Other Guy, Blankman's sidekick. The two take it upon themselves to hunt down Minelli and bring him to justice, making him pay for what he did once and for all.

Blankman is superhero comedy at its finest. It's also inspiring as it's the story of everyday guys trying to do the right thing even if it means putting on a costume and helping others. Damon Wayons and David

Alan Grier are hilarious and the chemistry between the two works well. If you didn't know any better, you would think they were brothers in real life.

This flick isn't your usual superhero spoof, though. It took itself seriously in that it wasn't tongue-in-cheek, but a deliberate superhero comedy with serious undertones. Everything from the social outcast that rises up, to the standing up for what's right in a world that's cynical and jaded, to going out of your way to help your fellow man, *Blankman* hits it hard on all points.

The jokes and humor are laugh-out-loud funny, the sad moments make you ache inside, and David Alan Grier's facial expressions are priceless.

Like I mentioned in my review of *The Phantom*, sometimes it's nice to unplug and watch a superhero movie that's lighthearted, easygoing, and loads of fun.

There's plenty of action and excitement in this movie to satisfy those looking for those things, but it's real strength lies in its heart and that is about two boys rising up to become men in a world that took away the one person they held the most dear.

As a fair warning, this isn't a kid's movie as there's grown-up humor, innuendo and some language in it so is recommended for ages 14+.

I've been a *Blankman* fan from the beginning and though it's been nearly twenty years since it came out, I'm still rooting for a sequel.

Captain America (1990)
Written by Stephen Tolkin
Directed by Albert Pyun
Runtime 97 min.
3 out of 5

Taking part in a secret super soldier experiment in the 1940s, Steve Rogers becomes the American icon Captain America. After an altercation with the Red Skull, he is trapped in ice for fifty years before being thawed out in 1993. Upon awakening, Steve must come to grips with being a man out of time and also that the Red Skull is still alive and is leader of a powerful crime family. Steve must track down the Red Skull, with each clue giving more insight into his own past and bringing him one step closer to his arch enemy to settle a fight that began half a century before.

This flick is your classic Captain America story, that is, his origin, his World War II beginnings, battling Red Skull, being frozen, awakening in the future and reconnecting with his old enemy who is still active.

I remember seeing this as a kid and liking it. Saw it recently a few years back and still liked it. It's not the greatest superhero movie, but it still holds its own all these years later.

It's very much Steve Rogers's story as he's Captain America for a little bit then isn't for a good while, then is again in terms of him getting into costume. As a kid, you don't care about story and just want to see the superhero. As an adult, you see the big picture so don't mind the non-costumed parts. It's a story about a journey, both for Steve and even for Red Skull as you watch Steve wrestle with himself for being from the past and how everything's changed, and also the different things he finds out as he searches for his enemy.

The Captain America costume is very rubbery, but it's way better than the one that appeared in the 1979 movies and looks pretty good overall. The shield rocks and when Captain America throws it, it's got that cool swooshing-through-the-air sound effect, adding to its power.

I was totally fine with Matt Salinger as Steve Rogers. He had that all-American sensibility about him, was naïve in the right ways, learned in others, and filled out those big red boots nicely.

LOOK, UP ON THE SCREEN!

This is a solid Marvel movie that was made well before the whole Marvel Cinematic Universe of today and should be on the shelves of every superhero movie enthusiast out there.

Recommended.

Captain America: The First Avenger (2011)
Written by Christopher Markus and Stephen McFeely
Directed by Joe Johnston
Runtime 124 min.
4 out of 5

It's World War II and the US Army needs to up its game in its war against the villainous Nazis under the command of Adolf Hitler.

Enter Steve Rogers (Chris Evans), a little guy from Brooklyn with all sorts of health problems, but who has possibly the strongest sense of morals and courage than any man on the front line. Unfortunately, due to his fragility, Steve is not allowed to join the American army despite multiple tries. A scientist experimenting in a super soldier serum for the US army notices this and offers him a chance to take part in a dangerous procedure that, if it goes well, will grant Steve superhuman-like abilities and enable him to be an ultimate man, athlete and warrior. Steve accepts and transforms into the world's first super soldier: Captain America.

Meanwhile, the first test subject of the serum, Johann Schmidt—aka the Red Skull (Hugo Weaving)—has come into possession of the Tesseract cube, a powerful energy source rumored to be from Asgard. His plan? Nothing less than overthrowing Hitler himself and taking over the world.

If only we had a super soldier to stop him. Wait . . . we do.

His name is Captain America.

Like all good fanboys, I saw this movie in the theatre. Having grown up on the cheesy *Captain America* movies starring Reb Brown and, later, the 1990 version with Matt Salinger, a part of me, I admit, was waiting for a repeat of the 1990 film (in the general sense). I was more interested in how *Captain America: The First Avenger* would tie into the then-upcoming *The Avengers* and this movie didn't disappoint.

The introduction of the Tesseract—which would be key in *The Avengers*—was real smart on the filmmakers' part because not only did it point to the forthcoming ensemble film, but also gave a quick link to the *Thor* movie as well.

LOOK, UP ON THE SCREEN!

Watching Chris Evans as Steve Rogers was fantastic. He really suits the role and played it perfectly. I wasn't sure how the once-Human Torch—all witty and sarcastic—would fare as the famous super soldier, and I'm glad Chris Evans proved he can play a kind of Superman-like character as well. Seeing him play both the small, frail Steve Rogers (facially, anyway, as someone else's body was used), to playing the suped-up Steve made the film truly a story about how our greatest power lies within as opposed to externally.

Likewise, Hugo Weaving as Red Skull did a great job, especially since playing villains is no strange task to Weaving (Agent Smith, anyone?). Even with the German haircut he looked different never mind later when his red skull visage was revealed.

The story was simple and, like the first *Spider-Man* movie, I left the theatre underwhelmed. After seeing it a second time, I saw it for what it was and really enjoyed it. Unfortunately, the end battle was anti-climactic. It didn't need to be an all-out brawl between Cap and Red Skull, but it felt brief considering these two are the heads and tails of the same coin. Some sort of super soldier/titan clash would have punched up the ending. Speaking of which, the ending of this movie has one of the best last lines to a flick ever. It was the kind of line I try to end my own novels on, one that finishes the tale but also has a punch to it.

As far as superhero stories go, the World War II setting gave the genre a breath of fresh air movie-wise as, thus far, pretty much every super flick to come out recently is all set in the modern day. Alternate times and/or worlds with a superhero figure are few and far between. *The Spirit* is the only one that comes to mind in this regard.

After this movie and *The Avengers*, I'm excited to see *Captain America: Winter Soldier*, which is presently set for 2014.

Catwoman (2004)
Written by John Brancato, Michael Ferris and John Rogers
Directed by Pitof Comar
Runtime 104 min.
2 out of 5

Patience Phillips overhears news of the terrible side effects of a skin cream that is being manufactured by the company she works for, Hedare Beauty, and is quickly silenced—fatally—for her eavesdropping. However, she comes back from the dead thanks to an Egyptian Mau cat and discovers she has cat-like abilities. Disguising herself as Catwoman, Patience seeks to learn the truth behind her own death.

Do you have any idea how excited I was when I heard they were making a Catwoman movie? I mean, it could be the greatest cat-burglar movie of all time loaded with super slick espionage, martial arts, sneaking around, Batman mythos references and/or cameos, strong-female-led action, cool costume(s) and more.

And then they made the movie they did.

Almost wish I could make this whole review two words—"no comment"—but that'd be cheating you guys.

This movie was not a Catwoman movie. I just don't understand what they were trying to do here. Had this been a fan film and some attempted new take on the character, okay, fine, whatever, put it online and let people decide, but this was supposed to be the real deal. She wasn't even called Selina Kyle in this. Instead, she was "Patience Phillips." They tried to jazz up what is supposed to be a very down-to-earth origin and give it a mythology of its own. Okay, points for trying something new and superhero or supervillain origins are often tweaked or changed for the big screen. What makes Catwoman as a character awesome is the fact that she's human, like Batman, and is basically his opposite. Not so in this one. She's got cat-powers and while it was visually cool to watch her jump around and scale buildings and stuff, it's just not who she is.

Halle Berry playing Catwoman is just fine. She's sleek, sexy and pulls off the part. The problem is the story is not very good, the costume is terrible—how slinky and impractical can you get?—and there's really nothing in this that ties it into the Batman universe. This is supposed to be a spin-off, but even spin-offs have a connection to the main source. i.e. the *Elektra* spin-off movie from *Daredevil*. Regardless of how you feel about that one, it's still a spin-off and is known as such.

This was definitely a comic book movie in that they went for "comic booky" as the feel of it. Felt more direct-to-video to me, seemed rushed and just fell flat.

Catwoman is an awesome character and was resurrected in *The Dark Knight Rises* in a much more real world way. I hope that someday—hopefully sooner rather than later—another Catwoman flick is made and they really try to get it right. It has huge potential. Sadly, it was missed with this version here.

Chronicle (2012)
Written by Max Landis
Directed by Josh Trank
Runtime 84 min.
5 out of 5

Andrew Detmer's got a tough life: he's bullied at school, his mom's dying of cancer, and his dad is an alcoholic. Andrew also likes to film things and his friend, Steve, gets him to film something him and Matt have found in the woods: a strange deep hole with a weird blue crystalline object inside it. After the boys develop telekinetic abilities, all bets are off as they discover exactly what they are capable of. The problem, however, is that with great power comes great temptation and Andrew begins to discover not only the extent of his power but what is deep inside of him. Soon, the group of friends are divided and one has gone off the deep end.

This movie is the boss. This is very much in the vein of *Unbreakable*, that is, the story of people pre-superhero or pre-supervillain, how they got their abilities, the discovery of their powers, the honing of them, and the ultimate decision as to what to do with them.

Filmed via "shaky cam" documentary style, *Chronicle* looks like a home movie but carries the strong story and special effects of a major blockbuster. Actually, it has a stronger story than most major blockbusters, but that's another topic. This flick is completely down-to-earth despite its out-of-this-world premise. By doing it documentary style, the character development of Andrew (Dane DeHaan), Steve (Michael B. Jordan) and Matt (Alex Russell) is through the roof and you care about each one, hope for each one, and get mad at each one when they do something you think you wouldn't do yourself. Well done, boys. Well done.

Telekinesis is the name of the game in this movie, that is, the ability to move and control things with your mind. While we've seen this power on screen before, this flick really gets into the potential of that ability from simply causing objects to float all the way to making yourself fly. Telekinesis would be the power to choose if one was presented with it because the majority of superpowers can ultimately come from it: flight, strength, stopping objects from hitting you, forcing bad guys to stop their actions, and more.

What makes this flick stand out is its intense study into what having such an incredible power does to a person, whether for good or ill. This is something we seldom see in standard superhero cinema as usually you got the hero or villain get their powers and already start using them based on their personality or because of how they're raised, or they are used a certain way because of a recent event. This flick asks the question—even answers it—does absolute power corrupt absolutely?

I've never seen a documentary-style superhero movie before. Correction: I've never seen a documentary-style superhero/villain *origin* movie before and I am curious if others exist. Will have to track them down because I thoroughly enjoyed *Chronicle*, was captivated by it, and it brings a level of realism to the material that even your most seriously-attempted-at-realism superhero movies can't portray. It's about everyday people suddenly getting a powerful ability with everyday people reactions, temptations, and usages.

Such a well done flick. So good. You need to see this. What *Blair Witch* did for horror *Chronicle* does for the superhero genre.

Highly recommended.

Daredevil (2003)
Written by Mark Steven Johnson
Directed by Mark Steven Johnson
Runtime 103 min.
4 out of 5

An A-plus report card brings young Matt Murdock to the docks to show his father. All he ever wanted was to please his dad and, as per his father's advice, "be a doctor, be a lawyer." Except, stumbling upon his alcoholic, washed-up ex-boxer father as a leg-breaker, Matt takes off on his skateboard in a hurry, only to accidentally run into a truck with barrels of radioactive liquid that cause him to go blind. But all is not darkness because he also mysteriously inherits a strange "radar sense" that enables him to see in a sort of X-ray way because of his newfound ability to convert sound waves into sight.

Him and his father vow to fix their relationship and their life, promise to never give up and be fearless, and embark on a journey to perfect themselves and hit the comeback trail—Matt via the books and honing his senses and disciplining his body; his father to enter the ring once more. With Matt by his side, Jack "the devil" Murdock makes good on that promise, but a fateful night in the ring changes everything and Matt promises from then on to stick up for those who can't defend themselves and watch out for the long shots like he and his father were.

Now, all grown-up, he's a lawyer by day and masked crime fighter by night. His name: Daredevil.

And he's not the only one who wants a piece of New York. Crime boss the Kingpin (Michael Clarke Duncan) is on the rise, as is his hired goon, Bullseye (Colin Farrell). Adding to matters, Elektra Natchios (Jennifer Garner)—a shapely martial arts master—has her sights on Daredevil (Ben Affleck) as well, leading us into a battle for New York, for vengeance, and for those who have been a victim of crime.

For some reason a lot of people didn't like this movie. I thought it was great. I liked the overall story; the costumes (except Bullseye's); the atmospheric New York City; the sense of darkness Matt Murdock carried within himself; Elektra's close relationship with her father; Foggy Nelson

(Jon Favreau) and his being a "come-with" guy—very enjoyable. There was a sense of humanity about this version of Daredevil that I was able to relate to on a lot of levels.

The fight scenes were nothing short of amazing, especially that barroom brawl where Daredevil clears the room. I remember seeing that in the trailer and just being absolutely stoked.

Who cares that Kingpin was black? So what? The dude's one of my favourite actors and it was interesting to see him play the bad guy as he's usually the nice, innocent one, but for some reason people didn't like the character being black in this. It doesn't matter, folks. He did a good job.

The whole Matt Murdock-Elektra/Daredevil-Elektra relationship was well-handled, in my opinion, and I particularly enjoyed how those elements intertwined with each other throughout the film.

If I was going to criticise a few things—and while I enjoyed Daredevil's gallivanting throughout New York—his spinning jumps and aerial movies were very similar to Spider-Man's (who made his feature film debut the year before *Daredevil* came out), and some of the stuff Daredevil was able to do was pretty farfetched. I mean, I don't care how awesome you are at acrobatic stuff or if you're more fit than Bruce Lee on his best day, but falling face first toward a window washer's station at lightning speed won't get slowed down by doing a somersault in the air so you could land on your feet. You'd break your legs and die from the impact. But whatever. It's superheroes, so I overlook most of the impossible these guys accomplish. Just goes with the understanding that superheroes can do things we can't, whether realistic or not.

That's really my only critique. I liked everything else. Wasn't crazy about Bulleye's costume. Would have liked to have seen him as more of a stealth assassin. I also don't read Daredevil comics so I can't tell you if this is a faithful adaptation or not. I know Daredevil's backstory and a bit about some past adventures, but that's about it.

I haven't seen the director's cut of this either, so need to get around to doing that.

Still a good movie and I'm proud to have it in my superhero movie collection.

If you like superhero flicks, you'll like *Daredevil*.

The Dark Knight (2008)
Written by Christopher Nolan and Jonathan Nolan
Directed by Christopher Nolan
Runtime 152 min.
5 out of 5

Where do we begin?

Three years ago, movie-goers wouldn't dare touch a Batman movie. I mean, what happened? Did you get your act together and deliver us one of the best Bat-flicks ever?

Seems so.

And now you've done it again . . . times ten!

Batman has made a difference in Gotham. Criminals are running scared. Underworld organizations are toppling. He has indeed become the symbol he set out to be.

Now a psychotic clown-faced criminal is tearing his way through the Gotham City underworld, quickly establishing himself as the Clown Prince of Crime. His method: death, and lots of it. His motive: madness. But is he crazy? As he would say, "I'm not. No, I'm not." And he's right. He's not crazy. This man—this "Joker"—is brilliant, and if he gets his way, Gotham will fall into his hands.

Unless Batman can stop him.

The Joker's reign of terror starts in the underworld but reaches deep into Gotham's social structure, various men strategically placed throughout the police, mayoral offices, everywhere. And they listen to him. Except for Gotham's White Knight, Harvey Dent, the do-gooding district attorney who's dedicated himself to cleaning up Gotham and taking down the crime syndicates that have oppressed it for so long.

Death reigns supreme in this movie. People die, and Batman is faced with the hard choice of becoming that which he hates . . . or risk losing Gotham and those he loves to this madman.

I cannot say enough good things about this movie. Going into this thing back in 2008, and despite the crazy good trailers for *The Dark Knight*, I wasn't sure if *Batman Begins* could be beat or even tied. *Batman Begins* was what put serious superhero flicks back on the map in a big, big way. It was what restored the faith of us fans in DC Comics and gave us hope that they started the journey to taking down their number one competitor at the box office, Marvel. And with *Superman Returns* being just plain poopy, I hoped against hope they'd at least get Batman right a second time.

And they did. They so did and me and everyone in that theatre were gushing with joy that not only was *The Dark Knight* as good as *Batman Begins*, it was even better.

Christian Bale delivered another solid performance as Bruce Wayne/Batman. The new suit rocked hard. Loved the detail. Though he was less buff than the previous film—why? who knows? You'd think a crime fighter would maintain a fitness regimen—he did a great job differentiating between the boring and dull playboy Bruce Wayne and the rage-filled-justice-driven Batman. My only issue was the voice. In *Batman Begins*, it was gruff, cool and tough. In this one, he sounded like he was growling the whole time and he had to *force* the words out to make them all gravelly. (And, FYI, WB, Batman's voice doesn't have to be like he's talking through pebbles and sand; Kevin Conroy proved that.)

Heath Ledger's Joker was utterly amazing. Creepy. Gothic. Funny, but not comical (like Jack Nicholson's was). Eerie, disturbed, crazy—delicious. What I loved the most was two things: 1) the clown makeup was just that: makeup. At first I didn't like this idea and wanted the Joker to have been a victim of an acid bath ala his comic book backstory, but after watching the movie, I see why they went this route. Bringing us to 2) Joker was a genius. It was his brilliant criminal mind that enabled him to quickly establish himself as a powerful evil force in Gotham and the makeup was his edge in doing that both in a scary-because-I'm-crazy way, but also it made others think he was *merely* a lunatic in turn making them drop their guard so he could move in.

Once more, I really dug Gary Oldman's James Gordon and seeing him officially become commissioner in this was cool.

Likewise Aaron Eckhart as Harvey Dent and, eventually, Two-Face—hey, he did a good job on both sides of the, um, coin. My only thing with Two-Face in this flick was that I wasn't expecting him to show up. I thought this movie would establish the Harvey Dent character in turn setting him up to become Two-Face in the next one. So, yeah, that part was a bit rushed but them's the breaks.

I enjoyed Maggie Gyllenhaal as Rachel Dawes better than Katie Holmes. Maggie's kind and cute, but can be rough and tough when she needs to. Worked well for Bruce's childhood friend/love interest, especially when that twist came that changed Rachel's future forever.

My only other little quibble was the whole bat-sonar thing. That was venturing into *Batman Forever* territory and we all know how that one turned out, but the positives of this movie more than made up for the couple of minor issues I had with it.

This movie is just tremendously good. Good fighting. Good story. Good stuff.

Very recommended.

The Dark Knight Rises (2012)
Written by Christopher Nolan and Jonathan Nolan
Directed by Christopher Nolan
Runtime 165 min.
5 out of 5

It has been eight years since the Batman took the wrap for the murder of District Attorney Harvey Dent. Eight years since the last time the Dark Knight was spotted in Gotham. The streets are safe, the police are receiving praise for doing a good job—except Commissioner James Gordon knows it's all based on a lie. About to come clean of what really happened that fateful night, Gotham is suddenly thrown into chaos at the hands of a mastermind, muscle-loaded criminal named Bane. With the city about to fall, the Batman must return to restore order to his beloved city otherwise it will fall into the hands of a sadistic genius bent on its destruction.

To complicate matters, a mysterious female cat burglar is working out an agenda of her own and her endgame is tied into the legacy of Bruce Wayne.

Will Batman rise from the shadows to defeat evil once more, or has he had his day and should stay in the dark?

Saw the midnight screening of this gem before it hit theatres all over the world. This movie is epic on a scale that is hard to fit into a simple review, especially since I don't want to give away any key plot points and/or spoilers.

The Dark Knight Rises picks up immediately after *The Dark Knight* storyline-wise, and eight years later in movie-time. Running throughout the whole flick are threads from *Batman Begins* and *The Dark Knight*, plotlines that reach their ultimate climax in what I have to say is one of the best endings to a trilogy I've ever seen. It's on par with, third-movie-wise, *Return of the Jedi* and *Return of the King*. All comes to a head as we're led down a deep tunnel into who Bruce Wayne (Christian Bale) truly is and what being Batman has done to him. Glimpses of his scarred psyche were hinted at in the previous two movies, but really get hit home in an emotional and powerful way throughout this final installment.

Batman himself also shines as he gets to show off his physical skill against a villain that can truly stand toe-to-toe with him, something we never saw in the previous two films. The battle with Bane (Tom Hardy) is realistic, strongly-delivered, and one where this reviewer felt the punches thrown as if they were happening to him. Yeah, it was that good of a fight.

The other Bat-flicks struggled with having two villains in the same movie. To be honest, I never thought I'd see the day where a modern superhero movie would have more than one villain and be just as good as if it had just one. Anne Hathaway's Catwoman is the best rendition of the character I've seen on screen, both in movies and on TV. She had to play multiple roles given her identity as a thief and work her deception in such a way that a lot of the time we weren't sure who's side she was on. I'm an Anne Hathaway fan, but this movie easily contains her best career performance to date.

Bane was a crazy good villain, a kind of cross between Joker—intelligence-wise—and Ra's Al Ghul—combat-wise—of the previous two movies. Especially since most of his face was covered with a mask throughout the whole flick, Tom Hardy had to act with his eyes in such a way as to deliver a performance as if he wasn't wearing a mask at all. It was something he did in spades. Bane was one of those on-screen villains that you were afraid of because he's that smart and that powerful and that sadistic.

Gary Oldman did an amazing job, as usual, as Jim Gordon, and Sir Michael Caine nailed it once again as Alfred. In fact, I'd be shocked if Sir Michael doesn't get an Oscar nomination for his emotional portrayal of a hard-headed vigilante's butler.

It'd be so easy to give away several key plot points in this review, but I'm keeping it vague on purpose because you simply need to see this movie for yourself. You might think you have it figured out, but you'd be wrong, my friend.

All dangling story threads from the previous two movies are resolved, the SFX did its job but the movie didn't rely on it, and *The Dark Knight Rises* had one of the best movie endings in history, to me, one equal to the incredibly-satisfying ending of *The Shawshank Redemption*.

Hats off to director Christopher Nolan and crew for the amazing stories and respect they delivered to Bat-fans everywhere throughout the entire *Dark Knight Trilogy*.

Go watch this Bat-flick. You must return to Gotham. You must.

Recommended.

Defendor (2009)
Written by Peter Stebbings
Directed by Peter Stebbings
Runtime 101 min.
4.5 out of 5

Arthur Poppington (Woody Harrelson) has a secret: when night rises upon the city, he takes to the streets as Defendor, a lone avenger on the hunt for the ever-elusive Captain Industry. Unfortunately for Arthur, he's mildly retarded and the line between right and wrong sometimes blurs. Though he means well, sometimes he gets in over his head, especially when his search for Captain Industry takes him into the city's underworld of drugs, guns and prostitution.

After saving the life of prostitute and drug-addict Kat Debrofkowitz (Kat Dennings), Arthur takes her in and, though at first exploited by her for money, the two eventually bond and he accomplishes one of his first objectives he had since donning the Defendor uniform: helping those who need it most.

Being a lifelong superhero fan, there are a few things, to me, that define a good superhero movie and *Defendor* had more than one of those things. It touched me on that very human level of seeing a sincere human being trying to make a difference regardless of what other people thought of him. Fear of man is one of the things I think holds people back from doing the right thing in real life. To at least see that attribute on the screen means a lot to me because it proves that people are still thinking about it even if it's just in a movie.

The trailer for this flick makes it come across as more of a superhero spoof than a serious movie, and this was most definitely a serious movie. Sure, there were some funny moments, but this movie wasn't about that, but instead was about a man who saw something wrong and did the best he could with what he knew how to do.

And he did. He showed us who Captain Industry really was: the villain that all of us have in each of our cities, the one comprised of drugs, guns and illegal sex that has ruined countless lives yet for some reason authorities refuse to do something about.

This movie makes me think of the real life superheroes that are out there (see www.reallifesuperheroes.org), those real men and women who don guises of other personas and do what they can to help us. Lots of people mock them. Lots of people mocked Defendor, but when all is said and done, they, like Defendor, do the right thing and try to right a world full of wrongs, bring hope to those who need it, and set an example that we should all follow.

Defendor is a fantastic movie and I'm really glad Peter Stebbings went ahead and made this flick.

Fight back.

Recommended.

Elektra (2005)
Written by Zak Penn, Stuart Zicherman and Raven Metzner
Directed by Rob Bowman
Runtime 97 min.
2.5 out of 5

After coming back from the dead and trained in the deadly art of Kimagure, Elektra Natchios is a killer-for-hire. Upon receiving her new contract, she goes up against a band of ninja assassins known as The Hand, who are also after the same target: a young martial arts prodigy with a potential for greatness. Elektra's past meets her present as she seeks to protect this young prodigy while also facing demons of her own.

I was in the minority of people who liked *Daredevil*, in which Jennifer Garner also played Elektra. When I heard she was getting her own spin-off movie, I was really excited because, while I'm not an expert on the Elektra character, I know enough to know that a film version would be awesome. We didn't quite get that with this flick, but that's not to say it was utterly terrible. However, what audiences expected and what they got were different things.

Let's see . . . I was happy that Elektra sported her famous red costume in this as opposed to the black one in *Daredevil*. Though technically totally impractical in real life, having her very-similar-to-comic-book-costume on screen was cool for fanboys and fangirls alike and, no, not for the reason you'd think. Just something about seeing a comic book character "as they are" on screen brings a thrill.

The fighting sequences were not bad and Hollywood's version/perception of the martial arts is always interesting as they tend to add all sorts of legend and mystique to them as opposed to their reality.

They got the gist of the character but didn't get hardcore into it, and it was clear this was just a way to cash in on the *Daredevil* movie that came out a couple years before. A solid story of Elektra's assassin exploits—even if you want her to fight mercenaries with a similar agenda—would've been a great help, but this flick seemed more introspective and slower paced versus something that should've been geared toward the action-and-suspense genre (i.e. a high profile target, like a president or something, then have that person tie into Elektra's mythology. Set her on the run while also giving her history and what it's like to be someone who was supposed to be dead, some in-costume Daredevil universe cameos, and you'd have a solid story). Just ideas.

In the end, if they ever went back and rebooted the character, I'd definitely check it out as the potential is there, but wasn't fully exploited with this outing.

Fantastic 4: Rise of the Silver Surfer (2007)
Written by Don Payne and Mark Frost
Directed by Tim Story
Runtime 92 min.
4 out of 5

Galactus, a giant planet-eating alien, is heading for Earth and he sends the Silver Surfer to scout things out. When the Fantastic Four meet this herald of destruction, all bets are off and it's a race to save the planet before Galactus can consume it.

What a great follow up to 2005's *Fantastic Four*. I remember when news hit that the Silver Surfer would be involved and that Galactus would be the bad guy I was beside myself with fanboy joy. And that trailer? Man, sweet stuff and totally got me stoked. Did this movie live up to the hype? Not completely, but that's not to say it was a terrible movie. It was every bit as good as its predecessor, but more exciting thanks to the Silver Surfer zipping around on his board and the Fantastic Four trying to track him down. That scene where the Human Torch meets the Surfer and the two quickly have it out? Yeah, sweet stuff.

This flick played up all the stuff that made the first one good, which was the family dynamic of the Fantastic Four, the bitter evilness of Dr. Doom, and then upped the ante by bringing in Galactus. Unfortunately, Galactus—while just fine as a concept—failed to deliver in terms of execution as comic book fans were really hoping for the giant space man with the purple helmet instead of the big haze of cloud we got. Some would argue that a big man that's larger than planet Earth wouldn't translate to film and a space cloud works better, but I disagree because Galactus is an all-powerful alien, can change size and could work as is if written well.

I totally dug Laurence Fishburne as the voice of the Silver Surfer. The guy can say anything and it'll sound cool (i.e. see his dialogue as Morpheus in *The Matrix* and its sequels; the words themselves are ridiculous but he makes them sound awesome).

The story arc as suggested at in this flick would've better been the stuff of a trilogy, starting off with the Silver Surfer's origin, how he got involved with Galactus, even a demo of him going ahead of his master to a planet other than Earth, the destruction of that planet then going to Earth, meeting the FF, and the whole planet getting ready to fend off this literally giant threat. So I feel we got the *Reader's Digest* version of such a story in this movie. It still works, but it could've been expanded upon.

As always, the SFX were great and they tidied up Mr. Fantastic's stretching abilities so they weren't as cartoony as in the first movie.

I totally would've been up for them to make a third movie, but with Marvel's Phase One plan no doubt in the works at the time this flick was released, we're basically going to get a *Fantastic Four* reboot at some point in the future, probably sooner rather than later.

I'll be there because I liked these movies and am eager to see how things will progress from here and if it'll be an all-out reboot complete with origin story, or if they'll sort of unofficially acknowledge these movies that came before.

Fantastic Four (2005)
Written by Michael France and Mark Frost
Directed by Tim Story
Runtime 106 min.
3.5 out of 5

Five people are endowed with superpowers after an accident on a space station. Four become a force for good. One becomes a force for evil. That's pretty much it.

This is a fun movie and I liked it. It had a solid origin story, some good action, and pretty good SFX. Each character was clearly defined, even stereotypical, but that's the Fantastic Four for you.

A lot of people griped on this movie. It was not bad. Wasn't as "cosmic" or over-the-top as I would've liked, but it wasn't a bad flick by any means. It was a great translation of comic book to screen and carried that vibe with it from beginning to end.

The invisibility effects of the Invisible Woman (Jessica Alba) were awesome, a sweet combination of complete I-can't-see-you-at-all invisibility with the glass-like, transparent humanoid figure so we can see her enough to know what she's doing.

The Human Torch (Chris Evans) looked like a man on fire, which he is, but animated enough so we can make out his actions, his costume, facial expressions and anything else we needed to in a given scene.

Mr. Fantastic (Ioan Gruffudd): at some points he looked like a real-life stretchy dude, at others the CGI was very clear (i.e. that scene when he stretches his hand under the door to unlock it from the outside).

The Thing (Michael Chiklis), arguably the hardest costume because you didn't want to run the risk of making him look like a cartoon character by going all CGI (as good as the Hulk looks even in *The Avengers*, there's still an animated quality to it), but you also didn't want bad prosthetics either. The Thing in this movie looked amazing and looked real. Well done.

Dr. Doom (Julian McMahon) was fine as is, his costume something like an elaborate cosplay. I would've liked more detail in the cloak, some sort of pattern, but the whole how-he-got-his-armor thing was pretty cool.

What worked especially well was the dynamic of family and all the love, bickering and craziness that goes along with having one. There was real chemistry between all the main players and it added a dynamic to the team that made the whole scenario believable.

What also makes the Fantastic Four different is they're public superheroes without secret identities, that is, though they have codenames, everyone knows who they are. While Iron Man did this, too, having a whole family who everyone knows who they are changes the game. It's also different because, unlike Iron Man, they didn't decide, "Hey, let's be superheroes," but instead it's something that kind of happens and they discover how important it is they use their powers to help people.

For me, *Fantastic Four* was a good movie that I like popping into the DVD player now and then.

Ghost Rider (2007)
Written by Mark Steven Johnson
Directed by Mark Steven Johnson
Runtime 114 min.
3 out of 5

After having made a deal with the devil to save the life of his father when he was young, Johnny Blaze (Nicolas Cage) is a cursed man. When the devil's son, Blackheart (Wes Bentley), comes to Earth in search of a contract that would bring Hell to the planet, the devil makes Johnny the new Ghost Rider and tasks him with killing Blackheart. If Johnny succeeds, he can have his soul back.

Supernatural excitement and thrills ensue in this paranormal tale about a haunted man facing his own demons—both internally and externally—and what it takes to be the Ghost Rider.

There're lots of ways of looking at this movie, everything from was it faithful to the comic to simple eye candy to story to themes to—well, you get the idea. For me, it was all right. I like Nic Cage because, well, he's Nic Cage and usually just plays himself, it seems. Sometimes he steps outside that, but in *Ghost Rider*, he was Nic Cage. Ghost Rider did look amazing in this, looked real. That first transformation sequence was insane! It's hard to sell the image of a walking, burning skeleton in leather, but they pulled it off here.

The motorcycle—trippin'. Can you imagine owning a hog like that? Know how many heads you'd turn? And if you could ride up a building like he did? Yeah, thought so.

The story's pretty good and carries its own mythology and purpose. The elemental demons that Ghost Rider has to go up against were pretty cool and tough to beat, and the effects needed to portray them looked real. It's amazing what Hollywood can do these days.

This movie got a lot of mixed reactions from fans. For me, it was okay. Wasn't one of those superhero movies I could watch over and over again. At the same time, it did do its job in getting me interested in the sequel, which is on my to-check-out list, so that definitely has to count for something.

The Green Hornet (2011)
Written by Seth Rogen and Evan Goldberg
Directed by Michel Gondry
Runtime 119 min.
2.5 out of 5

Irresponsible and party-it-up guy Britt Reid (Seth Rogen) is living the life as the son of the well-to-do publisher of *The Daily Sentinel*, but when his father is found dead after a fatal bee sting, Britt's life is changed. Since he never liked his father, he goes to the cemetery and, meaning to sabotage his dad's memorial, he and his dad's mechanic, Kato (Jay Chou), end up saving a couple people from being mugged. Later, Britt convinces Kato that the two of them should pose as criminals so they could get close to real criminals and bust them.

Kato agrees and Britt adopts the identity of the Green Hornet. His target is Benjamin Chudnofsky, a Russian mob boss who is trying to unite the crime families in Los Angeles. Soon the Green Hornet and Kato find themselves neck-deep in the city's underworld.

Sometimes it takes a criminal—or one posing as one—to catch a criminal.

I don't know, man. I was super jazzed when I found out they were making this movie because I'm a big fan of the 1960s TV show starring Van Williams and Bruce Lee as the Green Hornet and Kato. I thought, hey, imagine doing an updated version where it could be a mob story with all sorts of intense drama, action and be a kind of *Sin City*, you know, with Green Hornet being an antihero and all?

Instead, I got a goofball comedy out of what was supposed to be a serious idea. I blame Seth Rogen, who I usually don't mind. He was one of the writers on this movie so obviously wrote to his strengths versus what the character was really about.

The costumes were cool, the action was fantastic, Chou's martial arts was aces—but they got the Green Hornet wrong and took the gist of him and then did their own thing. Too bad. This really could have been a hit had they done the original series justice and then tweaked it for a modern audience.

Maybe sometime down the line they'll do another one and do it right. In the meantime, if a straight-up, not bad superhero movie is your thing, check it out, otherwise there are other lesser-known-superhero movies I enjoyed more like *The Phantom* and *The Rocketeer.*

Green Lantern (2011)
Written by Greg Berlanti, Michael Green, Marc Guggenheim and Michael Goldenberg
Directed by Martin Campbell
Runtime 114 min.
3.5 out of 5

When dying alien and Green Lantern Abin Sur is discovered by brash and cocky fighter pilot Hal Jordan (Ryan Reynolds), Hal's life is suddenly changed when the mysterious alien gives him a green power ring and matching lantern with vague instructions to "speak the oath."

After finally unlocking the lantern, Hal is taken to the planet Oa where he learns he has become Abin Sur's successor in the Green Lantern Corps and is also the first human to ever bear the powerful mantle of a Green Lantern.

As part of his training, Hal is taken under the wing of a powerful Lantern named Sinestro (Mark Strong) whose view of right and wrong is sheer black and white, and who has no trouble enforcing the law with lethal force. Turns out Sinestro wasn't the first to feel this way as long ago one of the creators of the lantern rings—one of the Guardians of Oa—disagreed with the Oan Council and set off on his own, discovering a new power, this one the yellow power of Fear. Now the superpowered being Parallax, this former Guardian wishes to take revenge on those who banished him.

As Hal learns what it means to set aside his own pride and ego and live by the sacred Green Lantern oath—In brightest day, in blackest night . . . —he must come to grips with his newfound power and expel Parallax's presence from the universe once and for all.

After the crazy success of *Batman Begins* and *The Dark Knight*, Warner Brothers and DC Comics were in big need of another hit after *Superman Returns* failed to deliver at the box office, and so they went to another DC hero: Green Lantern. Good choice. He's a kind of Superman/Batman hybrid in that Hal Jordan is human and has the qualities and struggles thereof like Bruce Wayne, and yet by wielding his power ring, his superpowers get up there right alongside the Last Son of Krypton in many ways. Whether this was Warners' reasoning or not, I don't know—

probably not—but GL was certainly a good character to try and take to the big screen, especially since it had never been done before.

In a nutshell, the movie wasn't bad. I liked it. It didn't change my life, but it's not the piece of garbage many folks make it out to be. It covered Hal Jordan's transformation into Green Lantern, delivered awesome effects, created a sense of atmosphere both about the Green Lantern Corps and Oa, and came through on telling a simple story that got Hal Jordan from Point A to B in a reasonable amount of time.

People complained there wasn't enough action or not enough stuff on Oa—but those kinds of things aren't—and weren't—supposed to be the focus of this movie. It was about getting the ring into Hal's hands and teaching him the ol' Uncle Ben motto of "With great power comes great responsibility."

I like how it took time to get Hal used to using the ring and it wasn't a case of him putting it on and suddenly becoming an expert on creating green light constructs. And once he figured it out, I enjoyed how his constructs were simple—the racetrack, machine guns, etc.—as opposed to something crazy or way too technical. Why? Put yourself in his shoes. You'd probably construct something you're more comfortable with than trying to create some big complicated airship stocked with robot soldiers with a zillion weapons and stuff.

The love story between Hal and Carol Ferris (Blake Lively) seemed forced though it did provide a nice bridge between the realm of Oa and Earth. Clearly this relationship was introduced for sequel purposes because those who know the comics know Carol Ferris becomes the supervillain Star Sapphire down the line.

I think in the end, *Green Lantern* did its job. Could it have been better? Sure. Could it have been worse? Yup.

Regardless, I like popping this movie into the player from time to time, and if you're a superhero fan, you should, too.

Green Lantern: First Flight (2009)
Written by Alan Burnett
Directed by Lauren Montgomery
Runtime 77 min.
4.5 out of 5

Pilot Hal Jordan goes for the ride of his life when his test pod is mysteriously transported from the safety of an air force hanger to a rocky desert only to encounter a bizarre dying alien named Abin Sur, who had summoned Jordan via his powerful ring. Abin Sur dies and Hal's world is turned upside down when he is introduced to the Green Lantern Corps, guardians of the galaxy. Under the tutelage of Sinestro, Hal learns to use his newfound power and witnesses, thanks to Sinestro's words and actions, that the Guardians of Oa—those who created the Green Lantern Corps and the green lantern power battery—have grown soft in their approach to intergalactic crime. Sinestro believes a more stern approach is needed and so takes Hal under his wing to show him that might makes right.

The Corps faces a crisis as the Yellow Element—the only force capable of weakening the Green Element, which powers the Corps's green battery on Oa—has been stolen. Should it be used against them, the Green Lantern Corps will crumble and the galaxy as we know it will no longer be protected and chaos and evil will reign.

Green Lantern, to me, has always been a cool character, yet he's also always been an overlooked character outside the realm of us hardcore superhero guys. Batman? Sure. Superman? We know him even better. Spider-Man? Yeah, good movies on the big screen. But Green Lantern? Wasn't he that green guy from that old *Super Friends* show, the one with that ring that does stuff and, um, well . . .

Green Lantern is an outsider character. He's known and he's unknown. I think of him like Superman, the difference being is he takes the ring off and he's a guy like you and me. Superman doesn't have that option because no matter what kind of clothes he's wearing, he'll always be a Kryptonian. *Green Lantern: First Flight* reminds us of that: that beneath the cool power ring Hal Jordan is just your average guy.

I really appreciated the origin tone of this movie and even more so that 99% of it didn't take place on Earth. Here we got to get a solid look at the world of Green Lantern, which is an intergalactic one and not confined to a bustling Metropolis or an eerie Gotham.

To see the Green Lantern Corps—all those weird aliens with varied green uniforms—really added to the scope of what the Corps is all about and a visual reminder that humanity's protection is only a small part of what they do. According to this movie, there are thirty-six hundred green lanterns, each with their own sector to watch over. Solid.

I had only a couple minor quibbles with this movie. I thought Hal Jordan dove into the Green Lantern thing rather quickly. He gets the ring and suddenly—BAM—he's all green and knows what to do. He also seemed too casual and calm about all these alien encounters he suddenly finds himself having. If that was you or me, we'd be freaking out the second Abin Sur showed up, green ring or otherwise.

Likewise, Hal Jordan seemed to be the only guy who got back to wearing regular clothes when the ring came off, whereas everyone else still retained their uniform. I thought the uniform came with the ring. Take the ring off and you're back to wearing whatever it was when you put it on.

Again, minor, but something I would have liked to have seen handled better.

I know that comic books and comic book movies are not as much for kids as they used to be. Once again this DC film has some foul language in it. Not impressed because it's kids asking their moms for these flicks. It's not like the old days where superhero cartoons were clean language-wise.

The action is great. The fights are cool.

If *Green Lantern: First Flight* is meant as a primer for the upcoming live action film, man, we're in for a real treat and an awe-inspiring experience come 2011.

This flick is solid, enjoyable and fun. Check it out.

Hancock (2008)
Written by Vince Gilligan and Vincent Ngo
Directed by Peter Berg
Runtime 92 min.
4 out of 5

Alcoholic superhero John Hancock (Will Smith) is Los Angeles's champion. The only problem is as much as the city needs him, he causes so much damage when fighting crime and rescuing others that the city also wishes they were without him. Enter Ray Embrey (Jason Bateman), a PR guy who's just been turned down again after pitching his All Heart logo to different charitable organizations. When Hancock saves Embrey from an oncoming train, Embrey offers to restore Hancock's image to the public while also giving a nice boost to his own career. When Hancock meets Embrey's wife, Mary (Charlize Theron), he soon discovers that him and her have a forgotten past, one that's already altered their future and will do so again unless history repeats itself.

Wow. This is a cool movie and a take on superheroes that's unique. Though an alcoholic superhero is nothing new (Tony Stark aka Iron Man is a drunk), making a guy who's like Superman an alcoholic is, and seeing the ramifications of that play out is something this superhero fan was excited to see. Not only that, but you got to see what an inebriated superhero looks like as he uses his abilities. The haphazard way Hancock flies shows one of the dangers of such raw power if it's not under restraint.

The mythology brought forth in this tale is well done and turns the superhero notion on its head, bringing in the idea of a race of immortals that had once taken the place as gods or angels throughout history. The fact that these superhumans were created in pairs, and that if they chose to stay together they would live a normal life as normal humans and later die, added a level of tragedy to this film that was welcome though tugged at the heartstrings. Sort of that idea of "what would you give up for the one you love?" And in this case superpowers if you chose to be with them. It also seems that these super pairs have a genuine love for each other so to forego that is a great sacrifice indeed and was something exemplified in this flick.

Never thought I'd want to see Will Smith as a superhero. Still have memories of him as the Fresh Prince of Bel-Air running through my head, but the reality is Will Smith is an incredibly talented actor and while he has used his default funny guy now and then, he's pulled off loads of roles where Fresh Prince is but a faint memory and him as John Hancock in this flick is one of those roles. While I personally prefer actors who've portrayed superheroes to only be that one superhero and not take on others, if you put Will in the upcoming *Justice League* movie as Cyborg, for example, I wouldn't complain and would certainly look forward to it.

Charlize Theron—I'm a fan. Given the complexity of the *Hancock* story—namely where Theron's character is concerned—I really felt bad for her for what she'd given up. She also did a good job of holding her own against Will Smith, who's a pretty domineering actor in any scene.

Jason Bateman is, well, Jason Bateman, but I like him so having him along for this super ride was super fine by me.

Hancock is an awesome superhero movie that gives a fresh take on the genre as it doesn't follow the traditional formula. Maybe in the sequel, if they ever make one. I hope they do as I'd like to see where the characters and the mythology go from here.

Recommended.

Hellboy (2004)
Written by Guillermo del Toro
Directed by Guillermo del Toro
Runtime 122 min.
4.5 out of 5

A baby demon comes through an interdimensional portal originally created by the Nazis near the end of World War II, but is rescued by the Allies before he could fall into enemy hands. Fast forward some sixty years later to the Bureau of Paranormal Research and Defense. The baby demon is grown up—now called "Hellboy"—and he works for the BPRD.

When an evil hellhound known as Sammael is unleashed, Hellboy and the BPRD are sent to stop it. What ensues is a supernatural battle between Good and Evil.

This movie is a superhero monster movie, two of my favorite genres rolled into one. You got Hellboy (Ron Perlman), the lone gunman type but with a heart of gold; Abe Sapien (Doug Jones), the intellectual who is a humanoid amphibian; Liz Sherman (Selma Blair), who is a distraught young woman with major issues and also has a hard time controlling her pyrokinetic abilities; and Trevor Bruttenholm (John Hurt), the scholar and father-figure who guides the group.

As an amateur scholar of the supernatural world myself and all that that entails, the idea of the BPRD really appeals to me as I think modern society is very close-minded on the subject when the very world we live in—never mind all that's beyond it—suggests that there is much more to our existence than what we can perceive with our five senses. Too many accounts of supernatural happenings to discount that. But that's not what this review is about, so onward.

Hellboy is an exciting movie with loads of action. Watching Hellboy fight is, well, just plain cool. Very brutal, and is sheer brawn mixed with skill. (He also wings things, too.) There's some real good humor in this flick, as well.

With certain superhero movies you could swap out the lead with someone else and wouldn't miss a step, but with Hellboy, Ron Perlman did such a fantastic job with the character that it's hard to envision anyone else. Kind of like how Robert Downey Jr. *is* Tony Stark or Hugh Jackman *is* Wolverine. It's difficult to picture someone else in the role. Perlman played it straight, played it tough, and played it fun all the while making you believe this big red creature is a real person with real heart.

I'm so glad they made a sequel and as of the writing of this review, there's rumors of a third one starting up to round out the trilogy. I, for one, can't wait to see it.

Hellboy II: The Golden Army (2008)
Written by Guillermo del Toro
Directed by Guillermo del Toro
Runtime 120 min.
4.5 out of 5

Long ago a war was fought between mythical creatures and humanity and, during that war, King Balor, leader of an elfin race, had an unstoppable Golden Army created for him, one that laid waste to humanity. The army marched and destroyed everything in its path. Amidst the piles of bodies and oceans of blood, the king felt great regret so a truce was made between mythical creatures and humankind. The agreement: the mythical creatures stuck to living in the forests whereas humanity could have the land. As well, the special crown that King Balor (or anyone of royal blood) used to control the Golden Army was split into three parts, of which two were kept for himself, the third given to humans. Also, the Golden Army was hidden somewhere on Earth in dormancy, locked away.

King Balor's son, Prince Nuada (Luke Goss), didn't like the agreement so exiled himself and waited for the right time to strike and take control of the Army and remove the humans from the planet.

Enter present day, where business flows as usual for Hellboy (Ron Pearlman) and the rest of the Bureau for Paranormal Research and Defense (B.P.R.D.). That is, until, Nauda resurfaces and begins slaughtering humans as he tries to piece the crown together so he can control the Golden Army and find out the secret location as to where the Army is hidden.

To add to the B.P.R.D.'s distress, Hellboy and Liz (Selma Blair) are having issues. She wants him more domesticated; he wants to remain free-spirited. Also, Abe Sapien (Doug Jones) is taken with Nuada's twin sister, Princess Nuala (Anna Walton) and, unfortunately, she is linked to Nuada so everything that happens to him happens to her as well. Nuala wants to stop her brother for what he has planned.

The B.P.R.D. seems to have met its match, especially when things turn south and the Golden Army rises once more.

LOOK, UP ON THE SCREEN!

I was super late seeing this movie. In fact, I just saw it prior to this review. It wasn't for a lack of trying either, but life happens and other movies come out and, well, the next thing you know it's almost two years later and you're finally playing catch up. Let me just say it was worth the wait. I was a fan of the first *Hellboy* and though this one carries with it the same undertone as the first, the overall feeling of it is different: the first one was more *monster*-oriented and this one was more *fantasy*-oriented. I felt at times like I was watching a cross between *Lord of the Rings* and *Van Helsing.*

Ron Perlman as Hellboy was pure awesome. I love the down-to-earth nature of the character plus the fact that despite him being a kind of rock 'n' roll tough guy, he's really just a big kid underneath all that red.

Selma Blair was feisty and dark as always, and she and Perlman had excellent chemistry in their Liz/Hellboy relationship.

It was cool, too, to see Abe Sapien get more of the emotional spotlight in this flick with him falling in love with Princess Nuala. At first I thought the dude was all about books and that was it. Looks like there's a tender heart underneath those gills after all.

The layered storytelling was great, and there was a sense of history to the Army, the elfin race, and everything on Hellboy's side of the fence. It wasn't just some standard good-guys-versus-bad-guys stuff. Cool beans.

The action was superb, hardcore and fun. The epic scale for some of the battles rocked, especially when Hellboy goes up against the big green guy that grows trees. Cool fight and Hellboy's big hero moment/pose on top of the hotel sign hanging onto that baby was comical yet cool as well.

Was this as good as the first? Hard to say. Tied for sure, though the first one is still my favorite.

This sucker's worth 4 and a half cigars in my book, though.

Recommended.

Hero at Large (1980)
Written by A.J. Carothers
Directed by Martin Davidson
Runtime 98 min.
4.5 out of 5

When nice guy and tough-on-his-luck actor Steve Nichols steps in and stops a convenience store robbery while dressed as Captain Avenger after promoting the movie of the same name, his life is changed and he suddenly finds himself as a superhero. Now with everyone wanting a piece of him, can he balance playing to the crowd with doing the right thing?

I got this flick on VHS *and* on DVD and it's one of my all-time favorites. Such a warm comedy that harkens back to a time when movies had values and superhero action wasn't full of angst and drama. Instead, this movie is the opposite and I don't mean it's a goofball comedy. It's simply loaded with heart and is about a man who constantly tries to do the right thing in and out of costume simply because that's who he is, no other reason.

John Ritter's amazing in this flick. He was amazing in everything he did and it's sad he's no longer with us. His portrayal of nice-guys-finish-last Steve Nichols is inspiring and it's oh so rare nowadays that you meet someone like that, but when you do, your whole day has been made better, if not your week. Sometimes even your life.

The story is a simple one, but one that doesn't follow the standard superhero formula and thus makes the movie the great one that it is. It's about the guy beneath the costume versus the costume itself and all the explosive action that would normally entail.

Without giving anything away, but reading between the lines, the supervillain in this movie is someone who made the wrong choice at the best time, and the consequences that play out leave you with a morality tale steeped in how important it is to do the right thing even when it's not the popular thing to do. We can all take a lesson from that.

Hero at Large is a heart-warming superhero movie perfect for a rainy day. Or a sunny one.

I love this movie. It's that simple.

Hulk (2003)
Written by James Schamus, Michael France and John Turman
Directed by Ang Lee
Runtime 138 min.
3.5 out of 5

You're making me angry.

You wouldn't like me when I'm angry.

In a lab accident, Bruce Banner (played by Eric Bana) is hit with a healthy dose of gamma radiation, the effects from the blast triggering the dormant bizarre alterations to his body done to him by his father (played by Nick Nolte) when he was just a toddler. Now, every time Bruce gets angry, the gamma rays still in his body course through his veins and transform him into the Hulk, a booming mass of pure green muscle driven by rage and fueled by anger and frustration at all those trying to hurt him.

Bulldozing everything in his path, Hulk tries to outrun those who want a sample of his tissue and those who want him dead.

Bruce Banner must face what he's become and come to terms with its effects on his life, especially those on his ex-girlfriend, Betty Ross (played by Jennifer Connelly), and the relationship with her he's trying to salvage.

This Ang Lee-directed flick was well done, all in all. It took a while to get going (the opening credit sequence was especially long), but once it did, things got intense, heavy and also fun.

This is a very emotional story. It's a story of domestic abuse, suppressed memories, obsession, confusion, loss and everything in between.

If anything, though, it was too emotional.

Hulk is a hard character to bring to the screen but given the time allotment he had to convey as much story as possible, Ang Lee did a good job.

This is not a good-guy-versus-bad-guy superhero movie. To watch it as one would be doing it a disservice.

The comic book-framed shots added to the experience for this reviewer. Likewise, the all-CGI Hulk, once you got used to seeing him (he looks pretty cartoony at first sight), was believable and incredibly, no pun, well done. The way his muscles rippled when he tore stuff apart or flexed, the sweat on his skin, his hair blowing in the breeze—Ah, all good.

This film is for true Hulk fans and for the viewer who likes the occasional monster flick or man-on-the-run movie.

Hulk smash!

Hulk vs (2009)
Written by Craig Kyle and Christopher Yost
Directed by Frank Paur and Sam Liu
Runtime 78 min.
4.5 out of 5

Two short films, one explosive movie!

Hulk vs Wolverine: Logan (Wolverine) is called in to a small town that the Hulk just ravaged in an effort to track down the beast and stop him for good. However, once the two meet, they go head-to-head and battle to the finish. Different phases of the fight trigger certain flashbacks for Wolverine and he remembers bits and pieces of how he came to be and his history with Weapon X (who also shows up).

This part of the movie is all-out-hey-bub-come-get-some craziness. Wolverine lets it rip and him and Hulk go at it like no one's business, definitely making this segment the more exciting of the two in terms of action. I mean, Hulk really smashes and showcases his raw power and strength and, I'm telling you, there's no holding back.

Putting Wolverine up against Hulk was a smart move because here you got this guy who's tough as nails, has a healing factor, and has an adamantium skeleton—and claws!—that make him near invincible. On the I-can-take-some-serious-damage level, Wolverine is right up there.

I also appreciated how they had him slice into Hulk versus just having the two slug it out. Frankly, Wolverine's punches against the Hulk wouldn't him take him far, if anywhere at all. Have him start cutting the Hulk with his claws—and with them being adamantium, they can do that—now Hulk finds himself in some serious jeopardy if he's not careful.

Storywise, this one was the weaker of the two, but getting a brief overview of the Weapon X program and Wolverine's creation is a plus for fans. Besides, Deadpool is in this and who doesn't love that?

Onto . . .

Hulk vs Thor. Loki transports Hulk to Asgard while the city is no longer under Odin's protection thanks to his annual Odinsleep. By separating Bruce Banner from the Hulk, Loki removes the restraint on the Hulk and unleashes the green beast against the unsuspecting Asgardians. Thor steps in to stop the Hulk from breaking in and destroying the city. The two battle it out in the realm eternal and only one can be the victor.

Straight off, the storytelling of this one was much more complex than the *Hulk vs Wolverine* segment. I appreciated that and liked how Thor was dragged into this battle as opposed to him just trying to get back at Hulk for something or simply seeing who is the strongest.

Sticking Hulk in the realm of Asgard as opposed to having the story take place on Earth changes things up for those of us not used to Hulk fighting in that kind of arena. Throw some complex emotions and Hulk's inner turmoil into the mix by way of honing in on Bruce Banner, and you got a good Hulk story.

This one focused more on Hulk in that regard whereas the other one seemed to focus more on Wolverine despite this movie titled as being Hulk-centric.

The battles on Asgard were almost as good as the *Hulk vs Wolverine* ones, but not as awe-inspiring. I did like, however, Hulk going up against multiple opponents in this as he took on the Asgardians.

The movie as a whole—I wish they'd do a live action version or something similar if they ever do a follow up to *The Incredible Hulk*. To have Hulk not just have the army on his tail but also other powerful superheroes would make for an exciting flick.

You never know.

Hulk smash!

The Incredible Hulk (2008)
Written by Zak Penn
Directed by Louis Leterrier
Runtime 112 min.
4.5 out of 5

Dr. Bruce Banner. Scientist. Researcher. Genius.

Victim of a Gamma Ray experiment gone horribly wrong.

Dr. Bruce Banner. Hulk.

And the military knows it. They were there. They saw what he became—a hulking, big green behemoth made of pure muscle, rage and power—and the damage he caused.

Bruce (Edward Norton) has been on the run from them ever since, keeping a low profile and doing everything within his power to find a cure for the gamma poisoning that created the beast caged inside him. And now he thinks he has one, so he ventures back to the States to meet a scientist codenamed "Mr. Blue" whom he's been chatting with over a secure Internet line to work up a cure. He also accidentally runs into the love of his life, Betty Ross (Liv Tyler), and the two are now on the run from Betty's hotheaded military father, General Thaddeus "Thunderbolt" Ross (William Hurt), who wants to turn the Hulk into a weapon.

They evade him for the most part until General Ross decides to supe-up his special soldier, Emil Blonsky (Tim Roth), and, once that super soldier proves not enough of a threat to the Hulk, Emil takes it on himself to make himself a greater match and forces Dr. Blue, aka Samuel Sterns (Tim Blake Nelson), to turn him into something else—an Abomination.

Now only the Hulk can stop this new mammoth creature and the two wage a crazy, awe-inspiring war through the streets of New York.

It's time for Hulk to smash.

I admit when I first heard about this movie I was leery. It was only five years before that Ang Lee's *Hulk* came out and I knew that *The Incredible Hulk* was meant to be a reboot, so I wasn't sure what to expect and, really, a reboot after only five years was just plain silly.

As it turns out, this movie wasn't a reboot per se, but more of a *do-over*, in that during the credits it quickly gave the Hulk's origin story and then got into a story of its own without referring to the Hulk movie of 2003. And to make things even more "separate," there was that oh-so-cool cameo at the end by you-know-who that cemented this new Hulk movie into the current timeline that Marvel's got going on in the movies, one that will take us up to *The Avengers* in 2012.

What can I say? This movie was way better than *Hulk*. More action. Cooler story. More realistic. This really was a solid Hulk-smash type of movie that didn't get bogged down in so much drama like the one in 2003. I loved Edward Norton as Bruce Banner. Not only did he look the part of a scrawny scientist, he also acted like one plus also did a good job conveying the burden he carries and the suffering he has to go through because of what he is (i.e. sometimes living on the street).

There was a chemistry between him and Liv Tyler, too. The two of them could easily pass as real-life lovers. This kind of realism was crucial in showing the sacrifices Bruce had made in order to protect those he cared about from the Hulk.

The sheer power shown by the Hulk throughout this movie was just plain awesome. The strength displayed was astounding. The coolest display, in my opinion, was when the helicopter Betty was in caught fire and Hulk clapped his hands together so hard it sent a shockwave/gust of wind through the air to put out the flame.

I enjoyed Tim Roth as the good-guy-turned-bad. He's always convincing. And when he became Abomination, the big fight between Abomination and Hulk was terrific: two giant titans going head-to-head, muscle against muscle, power against power. Fantastic.

The Incredible Hulk was such a great movie and made you look forward to any sequels or cameos the Hulk will have in the future.

Recommended.

The Incredibles (2004)
Written by Brad Bird
Directed by Brad Bird
Runtime 115 min.
5 out of 5

Superheroes used to span the globe, saving people from all sorts of calamities and stopping numerous supervillains from taking over the world. However, after an incident in which Mr. Incredible saved someone who didn't want to be saved and the superheroes were sued for not only that but all the collateral damage their superheroic exploits caused, the government forced the superheroes to go into hiding and created a superhero relocation program for them.

Now, many years later, Mr. Incredible is married to Elastigirl, has three superpowered kids, and is just trying to lead a quiet domestic life while also being unable to help himself but sneak out now and then to do good deeds for people along with his buddy Frozone. When an opportunity arises from a private party for him to once again don his tights, Mr. Incredible jumps at the chance and gets to be a hero once more. The only problem is this private party is not who they seem and has a deadly agenda against not just Mr. Incredible but against all former superheroes.

The bonds of family and friendship are tested to their limits as Mr. Incredible must try and stop this threat without getting his family involved.

Except, it might already be too late for that.

Wow.

Every so often a superhero movie comes along that does everything right. Great characters, great story, great presentation. In the case of animation, great voice talent, a great tale, great effects, great rendering. *The Incredibles* is an utterly amazing movie and is in the top ten superhero flicks of all time. In my personal top five, easy, and very close to the number one spot.

This movie hits all the high notes on every level. Superhero action? Check. Awesome heroes and an A-plus villain? Check. Completely relatable characters? Check. A solid story with an interesting plot? Check.

A stellar cast? Check.

Ah, where to begin? That's the thing with this movie: there is so much right with it that it's hard to decide where to start.

Okay, how about looking at a superhero story without the super heroics? Before you throw stones because I know there's lots of superhero-ing in this movie, the majority of it doesn't have that stuff, but instead focuses on the lives of a family of superpowered people and what they have to go through to keep their powers a secret thanks to the government making it illegal for superpowered individuals to show themselves. You got Bob Parr (Craig T. Nelson), who's just itching to relive the glory days and finally does albeit covertly; you got the homemaker wife, Helen (Holly Hunter), who's just trying to hold down the fort against a husband she discovers is out gallivanting with his buddy (Lucius Best aka Frozone played by Samuel L. Jackson) while also juggling kids; Dash Parr (Spencer Fox), who's frustrated he's got to keep his superspeed under wraps; Violet Parr (Sarah Vowell), who's frustrated in being in a family that can't be who they truly are; Jack Jack (Eli Fucile and Maeve Andrews), well, he's just a baby and does baby stuff . . . but with a super flare, of course. Throw in a supervillain who's motivation for being one is totally plausible—proving himself to the one hero who let him down—and, yeah, the heart of this movie lies in the people versus just simple superhero action.

When it does come time for the Parrs to don their new gear and become the superteam the Incredibles, they take all that character development with them and bring it to the streets as they fight Syndrome (Jason Lee) and put a stop to his evil plans.

What's great, too, about this flick is the immense amount of world-building thanks to the backstory as to how the heroes—or the "supers" as they are called in the flick—used to be all over the place and then how and why they were suddenly banned from doing their job with Bob right in the middle of it. It was actually his case of saving someone from suicide that caused the whole thing. (And *suicide*, by the way, a pretty dark subject for a kids movie.) You also got to see many of the other heroes that inhabit the Incredibles's universe, giving you a sense of scope that adds to the believability of the story and enhances the character depth even more.

Thematically, this movie is about many things, some of which are dealing with poor self-esteem, sacrifice, being true to who you are, doing the right thing at all costs and, at its heart, the strength of family against all odds.

LOOK, UP ON THE SCREEN!

The Incredibles is a movie that is highly recommended, a genuine timeless classic, and there have been rumors of a sequel for years. Director/writer Brad Bird has hinted at it repeatedly, but is also waiting for the right story to come along. To be honest, a part of me hopes a sequel doesn't happen because I understand the power of a good solo flick and how hard it is to do a follow up that tops the original. At the same time, we seem to have come to a place in superhero cinema where the sequel often is better than the first.

What do you think?

While you mull that over, go back and watch *The Incredibles* again.

And again.

And again.

The Invincible Iron Man (2007)
Written by Greg Johnson
Directed by Patrick Archibald, Jay Oliva and Frank D. Paur
Runtime 83 min.
2.5 out of 5

When billionaire Tony Stark accidentally awakens an ancient evil while raising an old Chinese city, he must develop the means to stop it. Creating an exoskeleton armored suit, Tony becomes Iron Man and faces off against the Elementals, four supernatural beings that can control earth, fire, wind and water. Not only that, but he must face the evil emperor, the Mandarin. Can Iron Man stop the foe he inadvertently helped create?

You know, I might be in the minority, but I just couldn't get into this flick. I found it really slow, had not much Iron Man, and wasn't big on the animation.

From a story standpoint, the what-it-was-about, it was fine. It showed Tony's origin in creating the Iron Man armor, had him go up against one of his biggest villains, and had high stakes. Just wasn't really my thing. I like Iron Man, don't get me wrong, and am a fan of the live action movies, namely the first two, but this one wasn't really my thing. To each their own.

If you're an Iron Man and/or a Marvel junkie, I'm sure you'd really enjoy this or at least like it more than I did.

Wish I had more to add, but there's really nothing more to say.

Iron Man (2008)
Written by Mark Fergus, Hawk Ostby, Art Marcum and Matt Holloway
Directed by Jon Favreau
Runtime 126 min.
5 out of 5

Tony Stark has it all: money, women, fame, and little regard for anyone else but himself, but when he's kidnapped by a terrorist group known as the Ten Rings, everything changes and he soon finds himself with a car battery connected to a magnet in his chest. Tiny bits of shrapnel from the blast that led to his capture are slowly making their way to his heart and the magnet is keeping them at bay.

The Ten Rings want him to build them a weapon and Tony knows that if he does, the world will fall into the terrorists' hands. He needs to find a way to escape and to do so he must create something more than just the weapon the Ten Rings wanted him to.

After inventing a metal suit with some crude weaponry, he manages to escape the Ten Rings' lair and return to the world as a new man. Taking his iron suit discovery to a whole new level, he becomes Iron Man and sets to right the wrongs of his past and ensure that the terrorists who tried to enslave him won't do so to anyone else.

Iron Man is a thrill ride you don't want to miss!

There's something about origin stories that I have an extreme soft spot for and *Iron Man* is near perfect in that regard. Given that Iron Man is a "human hero with no powers" ala Batman and it's his suit which gives him his abilities, he becomes instantly relatable (well, okay, maybe not one hundred percent as I'm not a billionaire, playboy, philanthropist like him), but I'm on the journey of life like Tony with my own share of pain and turning points. The movie's pacing is bang on and progresses "as if this really happened," which is a huge plus for a superhero movie. (I'm a fan of super flicks that come from the angle, "If this happened tomorrow, this is how it'd most likely play out." My own superhero series, *The Axiom-man Saga*, is based on that premise.)

The Iron Man armor looks amazing and real, which is a big deal because most of it is CGI. I'm glad they were able to create real-looking metal armor that didn't look totally fake. Likewise, to see the progression from the oh-so-crude Mark One armor all the way up the Mark Three was cool.

The rest of the special effects were out-of-sight, especially the ultrasonic flying sequences. Looking at the world from Tony's perspective inside the suit put you in his shoes—in his armor—and made you feel like you were Iron Man along with him.

This flick also boasts a killer soundtrack and score that gets you pumped.

Let's see . . .

Robert Downey Jr. *is* Tony Stark. Right from the first scene he lets you know who he is and what he believes in: himself. This carries throughout the rest of the film, but he also does a good job of becoming a changed man as the story goes on and the Tony we meet in the beginning of the movie is different from the one at the end. A lot of actors who are on supposed journeys during a story don't pull that off and usually come across as the same guy from start to finish.

Gwyneth Paltrow as Pepper Potts is dynamite. She's strong, witty and is one of the few people who can go toe-to-toe with Tony's narcissistic personality. Excellent casting for this role.

Iron Man was the stepping off point for Marvel's Phase One, which would later culminate in *The Avengers*. I don't think at the time anyone knew that *Iron Man*—who back then wasn't really known outside of the comic book community—would become such the massive hit it was, the franchise growing bigger and bigger with each outing.

But I can see why. This movie is awesome.

Iron Man 2 (2010)
Written by Justin Theroux
Directed by Jon Favreau
Runtime 124 min.
4 out of 5

Taking place six months after *Iron Man*, old shellhead is using his armor to maintain world peace and keep things right as rain for the world. Enter Ivan Vanko (Mickey Rourke), aka Whiplash, who has a vendetta against Tony Stark and wants to see him dead for the wrong he believed Tony did to his father.

Meanwhile, Tony's dealing with issues of his own, namely that the very tool he's using to keep himself alive—the arc reactor in his chest—is actually poisoning him, and time is quickly running out.

Can Iron Man defeat a foe hellbent on grinding him to dust while also saving his own life?

Iron Man 2 is a solid sequel. It's not as smart as the first one, but it's certainly not bad by any means. The idea of the arc reactor slowly killing Tony is brilliant. I mean, really, what do you do, right? Just wait it out? Unplug? Tell someone? Good stuff.

A lot of people gave this movie grief and I don't understand why. You got superhero action, superhero struggle, relationship tension, introduction of a new hero—War Machine (Don Cheadle, who plays James Rhodes; the part was originally played by Terrence Howard in the first movie)—and a new villain with a simple but decent origin story. Adding to that you got the breadcrumb trail that will eventually lead into *The Avengers*. The cool part is this subplot—complete with appearances by Nick Fury (Samuel L. Jackson) and Black Widow (Scarlett Johansson)—don't detract from the main story. Of course, I won't fail to mention Sam Rockwell as Justin Hammer, who's an amazing actor and becomes whatever role he is assigned. I love that about him.

As before, Robert Downey Jr. continues to amaze me as Tony Stark. He *is* that guy. End of story. Never thought I'd like a self-absorbed hero, but he proved me wrong.

Anyway, back to the action: *Iron Man 2* has got loads of it, right from

Iron Man's first encounter with Whiplash, to the big fight at the end where it takes Iron Man teaming up with War Machine to take out robots and a newly-armored Whiplash. What I liked was the realistic—as you can get, anyway—portrayal of what a suit of robot armor would most likely do and fight like if it was real. It was fluid, yet appropriately clunky and moved as such accordingly. The flight sequences were exciting, same with the weapons used.

What was also good was the humor. Aside from the here's-how-I-pee-in-the-armor joke, which I found dumb, every other bit of joking around totally worked and still maintained that this was a serious movie with a serious hero fighting a serious villain.

What makes this third movie in Marvel's Phase One plan great is that while it had its own self-contained story, it was part of the overall *Avengers* plotline. I loved how the two worked together but weren't dependent on each other.

Do I watch this movie when I'm going through my super flicks in my DVD and Blu-ray collection? Every time.

A major iron thumbs up from me on this one.

Recommended.

Iron Man 3 (2013)
Written by Drew Pearce and Shane Black
Directed by Shane Black
Runtime 130 min.
3.5 out of 5

An evil mastermind terrorist known as the Mandarin (Ben Kingsley) is wreaking havoc via a rash of bombings, holding the world in his grip. Iron Man (Robert Downey Jr.) gets on the case and discovers the bombings are initiated by people exposed to the Extremis program, something Stark Industries could've had ties to a long time ago, but chose not to. Turns out those Tony Stark knew back then are neck-deep involved with what's going on now, have re-entered his life, and are making things complicated.

While trying to pinpoint the location of the Mandarin, Iron Man aka Tony is also dealing with the aftermath of the Chitauri invasion of New York in *The Avengers*. Having trouble sleeping, he's been spending all his time constructing various Iron Man armors to help himself cope. This brings tension to his relationship with Pepper Potts (Gwyneth Paltrow), who he's now living with and is dedicated to.

Upon discovering the location of the Mandarin and his true identity, Iron Man and his almost-sidekick the Iron Patriot aka War Machine aka Col. James "Rhodey" Rhodes (Don Cheadle) head up against a battalion of Extremis-infected warriors and must pull out all the stops to put an end to their reign of terror. The problem is these Extremis soldiers are so powerful that victory doesn't seem likely.

Can Iron Man prevail against an army as strong as he is?

I'm not sure what to make of this movie. Sure, it was entertaining and the storyline was fine. I like the idea of making it a direct follow up to *The Avengers*, and showing how Tony Stark's world—never mind the rest of the world—had been affected by the Chitauri invasion and the presence of the other Avengers.

This flick was loaded with solid action, tough bad guys, cool tech, guns and everything else that makes an *Iron Man* movie a lot of fun. I just wasn't sold on the presentation. This might be harsh, but this flick came off as the *Batman Forever* of the *Iron Man* movies. I'm all for humor in even the most serious of movies, but it seemed the jokes were either too forced or too slapstick to make me take this flick seriously. And that's the secret with superhero movies: they need to take themselves seriously— even if they're meant to be a comedy—otherwise they'll never work. There was an awful lot of getting in and out of the Iron Man suits in this film, both by Tony and Rhodey, never mind Pepper getting a shot at wearing it, the President, the Extremis guy—there were so many suit changes that the novelty of watching someone don the Iron Man armor was quickly spent after the first three times.

This film was not directed by Jon Favreau, which might have had something to do with it. Just seems this movie was weighed down with not enough Iron Man and a storyline—which was solid in and of itself— that moved slowly. I realize Tony's aftermath and post-traumatic stress from *The Avengers* was the focus, but the same goal could've been accomplished had there been more Iron Man. I don't necessarily mean more action—as action-filled movies that are nothing but explosions start to finish get boring after a while—but perhaps him having a love/hate relationship with the suit because being in it nearly killed him at the end of *The Avengers*, or maybe take the robo-injections to summon the suit to a new level because he's trying to make himself super to be on par with guys like Captain America or Thor and have him deal with that?

The extra scene at the end of the credits with Dr. Bruce Banner (Mark Ruffalo) picked up on the bromance from *The Avengers*. A nice touch. Didn't move the Marvel Cinematic Universe forward in any way, but was nice nevertheless.

If you're a Marvel movie completist, then by all means, check it out. Likewise, pick up the Blu-ray when it comes out to complete your set. For me, I think I'm going to have watch it again and perhaps I'll warm up to it a bit more. I felt let down when I watched the first *Spider-Man* in 2002, but got more into it with subsequent viewings. *Iron Man 3* might be one of those movies.

Just think they could've done a lot more with it.

Iron Monkey (1993/2001)
Written by Tsui Hark
Directed by Yuen Woo-ping
Runtime 90 min.
4 out of 5

Like Robin Hood, the Iron Monkey robs from the rich and gives to the poor, but instead of wielding a bow and arrow and sword, he wears a mask and uses martial arts weapons instead.

By day, Chinese doctor Yang Tianchun (Rongguang Yu) is a physician caring for the poor and rich alike, but at night he's the Iron Monkey, a high-kicking do-gooder assisting those in need who are suffering beneath the rule of the corrupt governor.

Meanwhile, Wong Kei-Ying (Donnie Yen) and his son Wong Fei-hong (Sze-Man Tsang) come into town. Soon after, Wong Kei-Ying is captured on suspicion of being the Iron Monkey after being observed in battle. His son is arrested as well. In an effort to clear himself, he offers to capture the real Iron Monkey, his son being forced to remain in prison to ensure his compliance.

Soon Wong Kei-Ying and the Iron Monkey meet and, after going toe-to-toe with no victor, form an alliance that will rescue Wong Fei-hong from prison and bring down the evil governor once and for all.

This movie kicks some serious wa-hoo-hoo and I'm not just saying that because of the awesome kung fu sequences, but because of it's fun presentation of a classic story—Robin Hood—through the lens of Chinese culture, martial arts and fast-paced action.

Quentin Tarantino brought the flick over to the West and I'm glad he did. I'm 99% sure I went to the theatre to check out this gem and it soon got a place in my DVD collection once it hit store shelves.

What can I say? The fight sequences are over-the-top—wire acts, crazy fast kicks—but those are what make kung fu movies great and give the fight performances that supernatural feel that can't be obtained otherwise.

The superhero fan part of me had never seen a kung fu superhero movie, and when I compare it to the Western version of martial arts techniques that we get in our own superhero flicks, sadly, we come up short every time. I mean, this crazy, fast-paced over-the-top form of fighting is one of the main reasons *The Matrix* became so popular.

There is lots that goes on in this movie storywise, everything from the simple rob-from-the-rich-to-feed-the-poor angle to Wong Kei-Ying's tense relationship with his son, to commentary on oppression and what's fair and what isn't, to comedic moments, tear-jerking moments, to adrenaline-fueled action—it's a full experience, something that Quentin Tarantino said in an interview on the DVD that is common in Chinese cinema but not really over here in the West. I think we need to learn a thing or two about moviemaking from our Chinese friends instead of compartmentalizing everything into genres and niches.

If you love folk heroes like Robin Hood, or are a superhero fan, *Iron Monkey* should definitely be on your watch list.

Justice League: Crisis on Two Earths (2010)
Written by Dwayne McDuffie
Directed by Lauren Montgomery and Sam Liu
Runtime 75 min.
5 out of 5

The superhero known as Lex Luthor travels from a parallel Earth to ours and summons the help of the Justice League to take on the Crime Syndicate, an evil version of the JLA from his own Earth. Agreeing to help him, the Justice League travels to Luthor's Earth and takes on the Crime Syndicate, pitting the likes of Superman against Ultraman, Wonder Woman against Superwoman, the Flash against Johnny Quick, Green Lantern against Power Ring, Martian Manhunter against J'edd J'arkus, Hawkgirl against Angelique, and, soon enough, Batman against Owlman.

In a true case of looking in a mirror darkly, *Justice League: Crisis on Two Earths* is a super heroic and super villained thrill ride that gives you two Justice Leagues for the price of one!

Such a simple premise but such a cool story. Why not have the JLA face themselves from an alternate reality? Who would win? If you're fighting someone every bit as powerful as you are, would someone come out on top? What if they thought like you? Talk about playing with one's shadow.

There's superpowers galore in this movie as each hero gets to take on their counterpart and show what they are fully capable of. More so, you get to see what our beloved JLA would be like had they taken other paths in life as the similarities and differences between them and the Crime Syndicate are explored.

A bunch of other heroes make an appearance in this flick as well, guys like Aquaman, Black Canary, Red Tornado (a personal favorite), Firestorm (another favorite), and more. Kind of a throwback to *Justice League Unlimited* in that way.

Don't be fooled, though, as this movie is more than just a superhero/supervillain slugfest. It gets into the deeper issues, the big one being about choice. In the context of the movie, if every choice we make spawns an alternate reality where the alternate choice(s) was also made, do any of the choices we make ultimately matter?

This movie is smart, interesting, and grabs you from the get-go. The action is top notch, the animation is ultra sweet, and if these direct-to-video DC Universe movies have proven anything, it's that they know how to make a good Justice League flick. I can't wait until they transfer that same know-how to a live action Justice League movie. Can you imagine how awesome that'll be?

Anyway, back to this one. This is such a good movie and is a must-have on any superhero fan's movie shelf. You not only get DC Universe's all-stars, but the all-stars of a parallel universe as well. Like I said above, definitely a two-for-one ticket and definitely worth checking out.

Justice League: Doom (2012)
Written by Dwayne McDuffie
Directed by Lauren Montgomery
Runtime 77 min.
4.5 out of 5

Assembled by Vandal Savage, the elite members of the Legion of Doom—Bane, Cheetah, Mirror Master, Star Sapphire, Ma'alefa'ak and Metallo—are shown how to beat each and every member of the Justice League of America. Using the specific weaknesses of each hero, the Legion heads out to destroy their counterparts and bring them to their knees so Vandal Savage could implement the next phase of his plan: annihilating the majority of the human race so he can bring about a new world order from its ashes.

To make things worse, Vandal Savage didn't discover how to destroy the Justice League on his own, and when the answer as to who was responsible is revealed, the JLA is rocked to its core with the fate of the world hanging in the balance.

Man, I love this movie. It features an all-star cast of all-star superheroes going up against an all-star roster of evil supervillains. Finally, we get to see the villains stick it to the heroes in a big way and not let up until the JLA is down. And I mean *really* down. It's not often you see Superman on the brink of death, Batman humiliated and defeated, Flash completely screwed, Green Lantern a broken man, Martian Manhunter totally incapacitated, and Wonder Woman so messed up she doesn't know what to do or which way to turn.

This flick is based on the "Tower of Babel" *Justice League* story arc by Mark Waid, who is arguably one of the best comic book writers on the planet. I can't comment on this flick's faithfulness to that storyline because it's been over ten years since I last read it, but I do remember the overall premise and this movie delivered on that.

The heroes and villains look great in this movie, and it does well in showcasing their various powers and abilities.

It's also an exciting movie that is fast-paced, has a sense of atmosphere, a sense of taking place in the overall DC Universe—thanks to other heroes and villains not mentioned above showing up—and gives the JLA a threat that even they might not be able to handle. And that's the thing with a JLA movie: the threat needs to be so huge and so dangerous that it takes them as a team to solve the issue, and considering each one of them is extremely powerful in their own right, that threat needs to be mega huge, not just physically but psychologically as well. *Justice League: Doom* has that and delivers it in spades.

Also features the voice talent from the *Justice League* animated series so that totally adds to it as well, giving it a sense of familiarity.

Out of all the superhero movies on the market, this is easily one of my favorites and is good viewing for kids and adults alike.

Highly recommended.

Justice League: The Flashpoint Paradox (2013)
Written by Jim Krieg
Directed by Jay Oliva
Runtime 81 min.
5 out of 5

When the Flash cranks up the superspeed and travels back in time to right a painful wrong, the timeline is drastically altered and he wakes up in a present that's not the one he knows. There's a war raging between the Atlanteans and Amazons, Batman uses guns, Cyborg works for the government and Superman is nowhere to be found. Worse, the Flash no longer has his superpowers thus cannot travel back in time to repair the damage and restore the timeline to the one he knew.

Powerless and with no Justice League to turn to, the Flash must decide how he's going to change the course of history and if he's willing to lose someone he loves—again—in the effort to save the lives of many.

This flick is the ultimate fanboy trip for Flash lovers. He's the main character and this is the first time in DC animated movie history that he gets the focus. You got superspeed, time travel, alternate timelines, the Speedforce and more. Way cool and, frankly, it's about time DC took a break from Superman and Batman as the go-to guys for movies, even in the context of a JLA movie. With a new Flash TV series in production as of this review, I'm thinking this was DC's way of priming the pump, so to speak, to get audiences ready for more adventures with the Scarlet Speedster.

This movie's strength lies in two areas: the Flash, and time travel.

On the Flash: you got a quick recap of his origin, a real sense for what drives Barry Allen, multiple amazing displays of superspeed (especially that running sequence at the end), and a hero to root for from start to finish. I loved it. As a DC guy, I like the Flash, but this film really made me appreciate him and care for him all the more as it gave a strong face to his mythology and character.

On time travel: I *love* time travel stories. The more scientifically accurate and plausible the better, but I'll take just about any story that deals with time travel, parallel universes and butterfly effects. I write about that stuff in my own fiction, for crying out loud. Here, DC went to great lengths to explain the time travel in a plausible way and apply what we know of its possibility as realistically as they could in the context of the movie. Nice. The DVD extras that go further into this are an added bonus for us time travel enthusiasts and are much appreciated.

Storywise, I loved this movie and the twists and turns it took made me go, "Man, that's awesome," more than once. When I found out the history behind the Batman of the alternate timeline I went nuts. So cool and so utterly tragic. Perfect for Batman. And Superman's portrayal in the alternate timeline? Crazy! Putting all that against a backdrop of an Atlantean vs Amazon war added a breath of fresh air to DC's animated movies because, like I said, it was relieving to stay away from putting the spotlight on Superman or Batman. (Granted, Batman plays a big part in this movie, but in such a way that it's not *our* Batman but another, which makes it fresh.)

The animated style chosen for this flick I wasn't crazy about at first, to be honest. The small heads and wider bodies looked weird. It grows on you, though, and eventually you get used to it. The color scheme and bleak tone throughout added to the overall feel of what was a heavy story, thus sucking you in further.

This is not a movie for kids, though. There's a lot of violence and gore, adult themes and some language. While I appreciate "grownup" superhero movies, I wish these elements would be scaled back a bit so I could show my kids these flicks and go on super adventures with them instead of having to shelve the DVD until they're older so they can watch it.

From a superhero fan's standpoint, *Justice League: The Flashpoint Paradox* is a stellar movie adapted from the graphic novel by Geoff Johns and Andy Kubert.

Recommended.

Justice League: The New Frontier (2008)
Written by Stan Berkowitz
Directed by Dave Bullock
Runtime 75 min.
4 out of 5

In the fifties, the world doesn't know what to make of superheroes. Some of them are accepted and beloved, others not so much. When a mysterious entity known as The Center rises to thwart the planet, the core Justice Leaguers—Superman, Batman, Flash, Wonder Woman, Green Lantern, and Martian Manhunter—must unite for the first time to stop what is seemingly an unstoppable threat.

Based on the best-selling graphic novel by Darwyn Cooke, *Justice League: The New Frontier* is unlike any Justice League movie out there. For starters, it's a period piece. Nothing modern day here, with the story taking place between 1953 and 1960. Even more so, it's art direction is based on Cooke's art from the graphic novel, where each character was drawn in a very forties-style way: simple, with minimal muscle and heavy lines for eyes. No bodybuilding superheroes in this flick. And, of course, all the backgrounds, supporting cast and tech in the film were all time-appropriate as well. Even the "advanced tech" in the film was old school in its presentation and style.

The story was good—very much an origin story for the Justice League, with the overarching origin story being that of Green Lantern—and each character was faithful to their source material. The pacing was a bit slow at times, with lots of talking—there were a few moments where I was, like, "Get on with it!"—but at the same time, it being a period piece, TV and movies back then had lots of talking, too.

Not that talking is a bad thing. Just wished for a few more fast-paced sequences—not necessarily violence or fighting—to move things along.

Warner Bros. and DC Comics are amazing at their direct-to-market animated features, each one meant to stand on its own instead of where one story feeds off another. By doing that, they pick and choose the best graphic novels to adapt and don't have to worry about the baggage of continuity as a result. Doing *Justice League: The New Frontier* afforded them an opportunity to do something wholly original and deliver something that modern day audiences haven't seen in recent years: a superhero story that takes place in the past. After watching this, I wish someone in Hollywood would do a live action version of Superman or Flash or whoever, but set it in the past. You can still be true to the characters, as this story has shown, but give something fresh at the same time and, from a marketing and creative standpoint, give something original as a result.

Justice League: The New Frontier is a fantastic movie, and for those who want more of their favorite heroes but sometimes wish something new was done with them, then this is the flick for you.

Recommended.

Kick-Ass (2010)
Written by Matthew Vaughn and Jane Goldman
Directed by Matthew Vaughn
Runtime 117 min.
4.5 out of 5

Dave Lizewski (Aaron Johnson), comic book geek and nobody-at-large, always wondered why no one stepped up and became a superhero. People aspire to be doctors and firemen and policemen, so why not also want to be someone else who helped his fellow man?

After ordering a green and yellow wetsuit off the Internet, Dave dons the outfit and hits the streets as Kick-Ass, a superhero without powers, training or even a proper motivation to fight crime other than "what if?" The first few weeks are uneventful, and after his first attempt at stopping a car robbery nearly kills him, Dave returns more determined than ever to rid the streets of crime. Soon, after stopping the beating of a guy from a gang, Kick-Ass is all over the Internet and soon becomes a citywide celebrity.

Little does he realize he's not alone. Enter Big Daddy (Nicholas Cage) and Hit Girl (Chloe Moretz), a father-daughter team of real-deal vigilantes with a thirst for blood and matching guns to boot. Their mission? Take out the D'Amico crime family, their leader, Frank D'Amico (Mark Strong), having been personally involved with Big Daddy long ago and robbing him of the one he loved.

Soon Kick-Ass, Big Daddy, Hit Girl and newcomer Red Mist (Christopher Mintz-Plasse) are locked in a war that, hopefully, only the good guys survive.

It's guns, action, comic books and bubble gum in this adaptation of Mark Millar and John Romita Jr.'s graphic novel.

This movie is crazy. A good crazy. A special kind of crazy. I knew from the previews I was in for a different kind of superhero flick and, man, that was what I got. This was fresh, exciting, fun and new. Most superhero movies stick to a formula (origin of the good guy then the bad guy, a few tussles along the way leading to a big fight in the end, the stuff in between usually dramatic bits starring the hero in his personal life).

With *Kick-Ass*, though there were those basic elements to it, the one thing that was really hammered home over and over again was the idea that, yeah, Kick-Ass was functioning in the real world. One with guns, knives, average fighting skills and no body armor. Some folks might think the violence in this film was overdone. Personally—despite a few exceptions—I didn't think so. You try doing the superhero thing in real life in a place like New York and see what happens.

I also really liked how they dragged that fantasy of being a superhero into our reality and proved, really, that it wouldn't work. Kick-Ass went up against real bad guys. Ones without mercy. Without care. They'd kill their own mothers if they had to.

The lack of a costumed supervillain also helped this movie and ensured the focus was kept on the good guys. I particularly liked Big Daddy's and Hit Girl's origin. It was simple, yet bittersweet and, if anything, really showed that despite being off his rocker, Big Daddy really loved his little girl and only wanted the best for her.

In terms of the non-costumed scenes, Dave Lizewski's real life was extremely relatable (especially for this comic book nerd) and his high school years and mine seemed to have a lot in common. Except for the girlfriend part. I wasn't cool enough to have one of those.

This movie was fantastic start to finish. The writing, the action, the realism—truly cool.

My only thing was the profanity. I don't live in New York, but that was a lot of swearing and if people really talk like that in NYC, man, I feel sorry for them. (But, hey, I'm just a Maple Syrup-guzzling Canadian, so what do I know?) If they don't, perhaps the writers can pull back a bit on the wagging tongue for the next one.

Looking forward to the sequel.

The Legend of Zorro (2005)
Written by Roberto Orci and Alex Kurtzman
Directed by Martin Campbell
Runtime 129 min.
3 out of 5

In this follow up to 1998's *The Mask of Zorro*, Alejandro must try and abstain from adventuring as the black-masked crusader in an effort to keep his home life under control as his wife, Elena, now feels it's time for him to give up the mask since he's been Zorro for nine years. Meanwhile, a nefarious plan is afoot to stop California from becoming part of the United States. Soon the lines between the Fox's life as Zorro and his life as Alejandro blur and our hero must balance the two and ensure California's statehood comes to pass before it's too late.

I loved *The Mask of Zorro* so was super excited when this one came out. To me, it was one of those "what took you so long?" things. Well, I don't know what went on behind the scenes or why the delay, but I was happy when they finally made this movie. Due to being a new parent at the time, I didn't make it to theatres to check it out and had to do so once it hit the direct market.

It was all right. Wasn't as thrilling as the first one nor was the story as good. There was a lot of Zorro in this, which, of course, is a plus, but I think because it was more lighthearted than its predecessor I was let down. Sure, Zorro isn't a grim and brooding hero, but since the first movie was so serious, I expected more of the same with this one. That's not to say this was all slapstick and camp. Far from it. Just had this lighter vibe to it that I wasn't really into.

I think, for me, the romantic tension in this movie is what wasn't my thing. There was good reason for it in the context of the story, but I just didn't see how Elena (Catherine Zeta-Jones) couldn't just simply tell Alejandro (Antonio Banderas) what was going on and together they would take on Armand (Rufus Sewell). Perhaps relationships were different back then than they are now, I don't know.

The swashbuckling and adventure were fun and would make any male watching it want to put on a mask and get on a horse and go ride around. Kind of hard nowadays, but you get the idea.

The thing that makes Zorro interesting in this movie is the fact that he has a son. *Superman Returns* aside, what other superhero on the big screen has to juggle being a dad *and* a superhero? Even in *Superman Returns* Superman didn't find out about his kid until the end of the flick so we never got to see him be a family man *and* Earth's champion. If you were a superhero and had kids, you'd have to keep it a secret lest they spill the beans to their friends. You'd also have to face years of them being disappointed in you because you're always "working" and are never around. And the sacrifice involved on the part of the parent is also high because you're missing out on all these great moments from your kid's childhood because you're off saving the day.

I think this movie would've worked well as a third in a trilogy after some kind of high-octane swashbuckling adventure of a second flick. Then you can have your hero think of retiring and moving on instead of setting him up as a legend at the end of the first movie then suddenly saying, "Nope, you've had enough. Let's slow things down." What happened in between?

This is a fun movie, don't get me wrong, and is a good time for adults and kids alike.

I do recommend this movie because I think it's important the younger generation knows who Zorro is in this day and age of high-profile DC and Marvel superheroes and suggest parents show their kids this flick for that reason.

Any Zorro exposure is good in my book.

LEGO Batman: The Movie — DC Superheroes Unite! (2013)
Written by David A. Goodman
Directed by Jon Burton
Runtime 71 min.
4.5 out of 5

It's time for the Man of the Year Awards in Gotham City. The contenders? Bruce Wayne and Lex Luthor. The winner? Well, you guessed it: Bruce Wayne. When the Joker crashes the party, Lex sees a potential ally in his fight not only against Superman, but against all superheroes. They forge an uneasy alliance and Lex uses Joker's expertise in chemistry to create not only a gas that would make everyone vote for him in the upcoming Presidential election, but also Kryptonite. In exchange, Lex would provide Joker with a special brick dismantling device that is able to take apart shiny black objects, something Joker's all too familiar with thanks to the Dark Knight.

Meanwhile, Batman and Robin have their hands full with a breakout from Arkham Asylum. Superman shows up to help and eventually the Dynamic Duo and the Man of Steel discover Lex's and Joker's partnership. However, team ups aren't Batman's strong suit but after a little coaxing from Robin, he learns that sometimes you need outside help to come to victory.

Just when Batman and Superman think they've got Joker and Lex right where they want them, the sinister duo unleash a powerful force that will take the entire Justice League of America to stop.

If you've played *LEGO Batman 2*, then you're familiar with this story. This movie even uses clips from the game, but then fills in the gaps with fresh animation. So while it's kind of a rehash, it's a well-done rehash and, hey, it's LEGO. LEGO animated movies are few and far between and I hope *LEGO Batman: The Movie – DC Superheroes Unite* is the first in a move to bring more and more brick superheroes to the small screen. Perhaps even to the big one one day.

The animation is crisp, flawless, and well-thought out. The graphics are amazing and convey a plausible world made of LEGO, every detail somehow made from LEGO bricks. No small feat from a design standpoint, creating something so believable yet so . . . LEGO-y.

With a solid story filled with the right amount of action and humor, I'm glad I added *LEGO Batman: The Movie* to my superhero movie collection. Besides, the exclusive Clark-Kent-changing-into-Superman LEGO minifigure that comes with it is not too shabby either. Glad to have him as part of my Superman figure collection.

LEGO Batman: The Movie – DC Superheroes Unite is recommended for all ages. I loved watching it with my kids and I know you will, too. And if you don't have kids, then it's still worth checking out. Again, LEGO? Batman? Superman? DC superheroes? Yes, please!

Look, Up in the Sky! The Amazing Story of Superman (2006)
Written by James Grant Golding and Steven Smith
Directed by Kevin Burns
Runtime 115 min.
5 out of 5

Look, up in the sky! It's a bird, it's a plane, no, it's SUPERMAN!

Sixty-eight years ago this world turned a corner. In 1938, two young boys created a hero that would inspire an entire planet and someone whom this world would adopt as its own son. Jerry Siegel and Joe Shuster gave us Superman, the world's first superpowered hero.

Produced by Bryan Singer (*Superman Returns, X-Men*), *Look, Up in the Sky! The Amazing Story of Superman* is an in-depth look at the Man of Steel's history, going way back to before Siegel and Shuster created him, what led up to it, and what happened once they put pen to paper.

This is a remarkable documentary. It covers the comic books, all TV series, the movies, cartoons, even a hokey Superman musical.

Interviews with Stan Lee, Gene Simmons, Mark Hamill, Adam West, Annette O'Toole, Bryan Singer, Brandon Routh, Jack Larson and a host of others are peppered throughout, with the whole documentary narrated by Kevin Spacey.

This is the history of the Man of Steel.

This is the amazing story of Superman.

Go watch it.

Man of Steel (2013)
Written by David S. Goyer
Directed by Zack Snyder
Runtime 143 min.
5 out of 5

A sole survivor of the doomed planet Krypton grows up on Earth and discovers he has abilities far beyond those of mortal men. Once grown, he sets off to find out who he is and where he comes from. The answer is discovered in a spaceship in the arctic and Krypton's Last Son, Kal-El—Clark Kent—meets a hologram of his long-dead father, Jor-El, who reveals to him his destiny: to be a beacon of hope for humanity, and also someone who could one day restore the doomed Kryptonian race.

Enter Zod, a harsh general and one who has fought his whole life to protect Krypton and its people. During an altercation with Jor-El prior to Krypton's explosion, he finds out that Jor-El has sent his newborn son off-world and, along with the child, plans for Krypton's future. A battle ensues and Zod is sent off-planet, too, him and his cohorts banished to the Phantom Zone for rehabilitation. When Krypton explodes, the containment units holding Zod and his followers release them and he spends the next thirty-three years combing the stars, searching for Jor-El's son.

Locating Kal-El on Earth, Zod sends an ultimatum to the planet, forcing Kal-El to reveal himself to the humans and to stop Zod from using Earth as ground zero for a new Krypton. Zod, like Kal-El, is now powered by the Earth's yellow sun and is empowered with superabilities. An enormous battle ensues between Krypton's general and Kal-El, the fate of the Earth hanging in the balance.

What can I say? This movie is mind blowing! It's epic, it's incredible. So much was riding on this film to deliver a Superman movie that would captivate audiences and restore the Man of Steel to his rightful place as king of the superheroes. *Man of Steel* does just that and then some, bringing with it the awesome sci-fi factors of *Star Wars* to the dense storytelling of *The Dark Knight Trilogy*.

There has never, ever been a superhero movie like this before. Henry Cavill as Superman nailed the part. He's a nice guy, a caring guy, but he's dead serious about doing the right thing and exudes the confidence that only one who has sold himself out for the good of all can portray. He did something that was never done before by any other Superman actor: showing Clark Kent *before* he was Superman or even the bumbling reporter of the *Daily Planet*. (I'm referring to the movies, not *Smallville*). In fact, he's this version of Clark Kent for nearly the whole movie. You see him making the big decisions, weighing his upbringing against this new task of saving the world that was suddenly dropped on his lap. You journey along with him as he wrestles with his being different and how those differences apply not just to his life, but to the lives of others.

As Superman, he's *the* Superman. I never thought Christopher Reeve's performance could be outdone, but Henry Cavill matches, if not exceeds, what Mr. Reeve brought to the character. Cavill's Superman is one hundred percent devoted to staying true to who he is, his abilities, his upbringing, his quest for truth and justice, and for putting his foot down both with men and rebel Kryptonians when needed. I can't really comment on his reporter Clark persona because that's not a big role in this movie. I hope, however, it will be in the sequel and we'll see plenty of Lois and Clark interaction in the next one, especially after the way the Lois and Clark relationship is portrayed in this movie. You'll have to see for yourself for what I mean.

Michael Shannon as Zod was crazy good. The guy can act and his Zod is much different than Terrence Stamp's. Yes, both are ruthless, but whereas Stamp's Zod was more about power grabbing and his desire to rule, Shannon's is about giving his all to restore the former glory of Krypton at any cost, even if that means eradicating all of Earth's population to do it. The best villain is always the villain you accidently find yourself rooting for, and that happened to me throughout this movie. Every so often I felt for Zod and understood what he was trying to accomplish. It made sense and made me consider that maybe if I was in his shoes I would've done the same thing or something similar.

Amy Adams as Lois Lane was a good choice. I wasn't sure at first, as I know Amy Adams as more of the happy-go-lucky girl from other movies far removed from the superhero genre—though she was in one episode of *Smallville* during its first season—but she sold me on the part and she reminded me of the Lois Lanes from the old cartoons: warm, but cut and dry; funny, but serious about what she does and her desire to go the distance to get a story.

The action in this movie was crazy huge. The bar has been set so high in terms of superhero cinema in recent years and *Man of Steel* makes every superhero movie that's come before it look like a puppet show by comparison. The wide-scale destruction wrought by Superman and Zod—never mind Zod's right-hand-woman Faora and the other rebel Kryptonians—is what you'd expect if people with god-like powers let loose in an all-out brawl across a city. And the speed, man, the speed! Normally superspeed is shown as either a big blur or done in slo-mo, with the superspeedsters moving quickly while everyone else is frozen. In this one, you see Superman et al. zipping around, pausing, breaking sound barriers, and bringing the viewer along as if we're in his boots the whole time and experiencing the thrill of superspeed ourselves.

The way Superman flies in this is unlike any other portrayal before, and while I loved how he flies in the other movies and TV shows, in this one he seems to hurl himself through the air at times, while at others flies with precision and care. The heat vision effect in this was stellar, too. The glow beneath the skin around the eyes and to see the veins beneath its surface made it all the more menacing. The superhearing and X-ray vision were familiar territory to those who've watched *Smallville*, but there was no all-out X-ray vision where everything was dark blue and white.

The fighting between Superman and Zod was serious business and was truly a portrayal of two warriors going toe-to-toe and not just wrestling or tapping each other out. It was one crazy hard blow after another, some slow, some rapid, even some in the sky! Insane! So many times I was blown away and just going "Wow, wow, wow!" Zod fought with the skill of a trained warrior, whereas Superman fought with brute force.

Man of Steel is a crazy good movie with a strong story, an incredible cast, and superhero action that has now become the benchmark for anything to follow. To be honest, I don't know if it can be followed. Hopefully in *Man of Steel 2*.

Super recommended.

The Mask of Zorro (1998)
Written by John Eskow, Ted Elliott and Terry Rossio
Directed by Martin Campbell
Runtime 136 min.
4 out of 5

A small-time thief's brother is killed before his eyes. Wanting to exact revenge against the soldier that killed him, Alejandro Murrieta seeks him out only to run into the original Zorro who is now retired. Knowing that if Alejandro tried to kill the soldier right away that he would only get himself killed, he decides to train Alejandro as the new Zorro and use him to stop the evil Rafael Montero from getting rich off the backs of the people and bring freedom to California once and for all.

I was introduced to Zorro when I was a kid by my dad. Watched the movies, was Zorro for Halloween in grade two, played dress-up around the house—I've always had a soft spot for the swordsman in black. Even dressed up as him again at Halloween eleven years ago.

He's the historical Batman—side note: depending which Batman origin you read, the movie theatre that Bruce Wayne and his parents left that fateful night was showing a Zorro movie—and packs a punch as deadly as the best of heroes.

This movie was the first time I saw Zorro on the big screen. What a cool opening with him walking against a spotlit backdrop and doing his famous Z-slash across the screen. And they got right into the action, too, showing us the first generation Zorro's last adventure and using that as a catalyst to the main story to bring in a new one.

I was especially impressed with the swordplay in this. I mean, it had to be good, right, because that's Zorro's thing. There was no way the filmmakers would fall short in this area, above all else. The costume looked good, too, and they didn't try to be all fancy and stylize the thing. They kept it simple just like it would've been in long-ago California.

The writing was real good, with a strong story. The tragedy of Don Diego de la Vega (Anthony Hopkins) is what made the tale. You got this guy who's given it all for the people of California and then just when he thought his mission was through, everything else that he's held dear is taken from him as well. To see him endure such emotional pain raises the hero bar because being a hero goes beyond the physical. There has to be a cost, some sort of sacrifice and/or loss.

Which brings us to the new Zorro, Alejandro Murrieta (Antonio Banderas). First, Mr. Banderas was the only choice for the role, in my opinion. Aside from casting an unknown, what other famous Spanish actor does Hollywood have to offer who has the charm, good looks and charisma needed to play Zorro's alter ego never mind the black swordsman himself? Throw that together with Banderas's acting chops and you got a Zorro who was dead serious at the right moments, witty in others, and played it straight throughout.

Of course, there had to be a love interest and Catherine Zeta-Jones filled in the role of Elena, Diego's daughter. She did fine and conducted a fine balance between a strong and fiery woman with a dainty feminine side.

I've said it in other reviews and I'll say it here: I like origin stories. What makes this one special is it's not just a how-Zorro-came-to-be movie, but a passing-of-the-torch one as well, giving you Zorro lore from start to finish and opening the door for a sequel, which ended up coming some seven years later.

I know there's plans to reboot the character, but for right now, this movie's a favorite of mine.

With a great soundtrack, great story and solid acting, *The Mask of Zorro* is a recommended flick in my books.

The Meteor Man (1993)
Written by Robert Townsend
Directed by Robert Townsend
Runtime 100 min.
3.5 out of 5

When a school teacher is accidentally struck by a strange, green glowing meteor, he is endowed with superpowers. Just in the nick of time, too, because a street gang called the Golden Lords have terrorized his neighborhood. Now, with the help of super abilities from the green shimmering rock, he's able to take a stand for his neighborhood and what he believes in.

I saw this movie when I was a kid. I remember seeing it at the local Pick-A-Flick and renting it. What I got was a sincere, heart-warming tale about a down-and-out neighborhood struggling to keep going while crime and violence ravaged its streets. Enter Jefferson Reed (Robert Townsend), a well-meaning and kind man who happens to be at the wrong place at the wrong time. Once the meteor gives him superpowers, he takes on the gangs and, at the behest of his own parents, also takes on the identity of Meteor Man and becomes the neighborhood's champion.

While not a serious superhero movie—there's plenty of humor to go around—*The Meteor Man* is not all-out goofy like *Blankman*, and instead takes a kind of tongue-in-cheek approach to the genre while also telling a story about strength in numbers, standing up for yourself, and simply saying no to being a passive observer of evil.

This flick is also—and I really don't know how to phrase it so excuse me—a "black" movie, with pretty much an all-black cast. I loved that part of it and there were so many recognizable actors: Bill Cosby, James Earle Jones, Don Cheadle, Sinbad and more. It's strange because I don't get that sense of community and warmth from watching flicks with all-white casts. Anyway, that's just an aside.

The Meteor Man, also written and directed by Robert Townsend and not just starring him as the titular character, was done at a time before superheroes on the screen were all dark and serious, where there had to be non-stop action and all kinds of special effects and fancy costumes. And you know what? It totally worked.

This movie is a memorable one because of the messages and themes running through it and I advise it to be on the serious superhero collector's movie shelf.

My Super Ex-girlfriend (2006)
Written by Don Payne
Directed by Ivan Reitman
Runtime 95 min.
4 out of 5

What would you do if you found out the woman you were seeing was actually a superhero? It's exactly what happens to Matt Saunders (Luke Wilson) when he discovers his shy but very controlling girlfriend, Jenny Johnson (Uma Thurman), is really G-Girl. Aside from being able to fly, bend steel bars with her bare hands, shoot lasers from her eyes and a host of other classic powers, she's also every guy's nightmare girlfriend and soon Matt can't take it anymore and breaks up with her. While he tries to get on with his life—which is way easier thanks to Hannah (Anna Farris), a pretty blonde in his office with whom he's got good chemistry—Jenny's not having so easy a time and makes his life a living hell, barraging him with super trouble and threats that only a super ex-girlfriend can bring. Meanwhile, G-Girl's arch nemesis, Professor Bedlam (Eddie Izzard), has his own plans for G-Girl and seeks to strip her of her powers once and for all.

It's good times, lots of laughs and loads of nods to the metahuman genre in this superhero romance comedy that you're sure to love.

I'm not big on romantic comedies. You've seen one, you've pretty much seen them all. However, there are exceptions and, for me, putting a new twist on them is the way to get this viewer's attention. If you make that twist superheroes, you've definitely caught my eye and *My Super Ex-girlfriend* does just that. While superhero romance is explored in the comics, it's never intentionally explored on the big screen. While modern day superhero movies do have romantic elements or a romantic subplot, it's never in the foreground—until now. By adding a comedic element, you take the risk of ruining the genre by making it too tongue-in-cheek or campy. Not so in this flick. Sure, there are a few silly moments, but on the whole, the genre is still treated with respect and taken seriously in the context of the film.

Uma Thurman is one of my favorite actresses. She's extremely versatile and is quite the chameleon. Seeing her both as the sleek and strong G-Girl and then as her Clark Kent-ish opposite Jenny Johnson shows she can play both sides of the same coin. More so, she also—whether intentionally or not, I don't know—knows how to stand the coin on edge, and that is portray that hero while not in their public civilian identity but also not in their super one as well. It's the side of a superhero character you don't often see and, interestingly, it's this side of the Jenny/G-Girl character that makes up most of the screen time in this flick. As a writer of superheroes myself (see *The Axiom-man Saga*), it's this side of the hero that most intrigues me because it's the side where they're just being themselves without having to put on a show for the public heroically or in disguise.

Luke Wilson—he's Luke Wilson. At least out of all the movies I've seen him in, he's, well, Luke Wilson, the soft-spoken awkward nice guy with a bit of wit. Such a character worked well to play opposite Jenny Johnson's crazed tendencies. Sort of the whole straight-man side of the comedy duo equation.

This movie is special in that it stands out amongst superhero comedies because it takes itself seriously while still being funny, and is able to make you suspend all disbelief for its hour-and-a-half runtime.

If you're looking for something lighthearted, but something super, *My Super Ex-girlfriend* should be at the top of your list.

Mystery Men (1999)
Written by Neil Cuthbert
Directed by Kinka Usher
Runtime 121 min.
4 out of 5

Captain Amazing (Greg Kinnear) is the hero of Champion City, but when he's kidnapped by the evil Casanova Frankenstein (Geoffrey Rush), a ragtag team of wannabe superheroes must rise to the occasion and thwart Casanova's plan before it's too late. That is, if they don't screw things up first.

If there ever was a *Seinfeld* of superhero movies, this would be it. What I mean is, it's a blend of everyday people doing super stuff while still dealing with the mundane of everyday life. The humor is overt in some places ala Kramer, and utterly-subtle-yet-brilliant in others (i.e. When the Shoveler hosts a superhero recruitment party in his backyard, his wife tells him she'll divorce him if one person vomits in their pool and he replies deadpan: "That's fair.").

This movie was a strange hybrid of wannabe-superheroes-from-our-world living in a comic book world. Normally, those two "realities" don't collide in superhero stories, but they did here and thus became the crux of the story: guys and girls who want to be heroes but don't have the chops to cut it in a reality where you need to be super to survive.

At the same time, *Mystery Men* was meant to be a comedy as the rogues gallery were very '60s *Batman*: the Frat Boys, the Disco Boys, the Suits, and others. Strangely, they were led by a leader who was much more competent and had the smarts to devise a plausible plan to take over the city.

As a comic book and superhero fan, I appreciated the nods to comicdom and its characters, namely when they discuss how Lance Hunt couldn't be Captain Amazing because: "Lance Hunt wears glasses, Captain Amazing *doesn't* wear glasses." Nice commentary on the how-does-anyone-not-know-Clark-Kent-is-Superman debate.

The casting is perfect. Ben Stiller as Mr. Furious, William H. Macy as the Shoveler, Paul Reubens as the Spleen, Janeane Garofalo as the

Bowler, Hank Azaria as the Blue Raja, Kel Mitchell as Invisible Boy and Wes Studi as the Sphinx. They all played it straight, which was what sold it given that they're really ridiculous characters—farting as a superpower?—and made you feel for these guys and cheer them on as they bumbled their way through their adventure.

I've said it before that I like lighthearted superhero movies, and what makes this one work is that while it's a comedy, it's not a parody like *Superhero Movie*, for example. It's just simply fun.

And fun is good.

Recommended.

The Phantom (1996)
Written by Jeffrey Boam
Directed by Simon Wincer
Runtime 100 min.
3.5 out of 5

A ship taken over by pirates. The death of a father. A young boy thrown overboard. Washing up on the shore of the Island of Bengalla. A strange ritual and a vow. When that boy grew up and became a man, he became the Phantom.

Centuries later, this boy's descendant—the 21st Phantom (Billy Zane)—is protecting his beloved jungle when thieves steal a sacred skull from a lost treasure trove. The Phantom learns the significance of the skull and discovers it is one of three and should someone ever possess all three, they would have ultimate power. Trailing the stolen skull to New York, the Phantom, now under his civilian guise of Kit Walker, seeks to track down the remaining skulls. While there, he reconnects with his old flame, Diana Palmer (Kirsty Swanson), and the two need to reconcile past differences while Kit learns the location of the second skull. Meanwhile, evil businessman Xander Drax (Treat Williams), in cahoots with the Sengh Brotherhood, a band of pirates—the descendants of the same pirates that were responsible for sinking the ship of the father of the first Phantom—wants the skulls for himself. Drax, too, discovers the location of the second skull at the same time Kit and Diana do and after a failed attempt at disposing of Kit, kidnaps Diana and takes her to the location of the third: an uncharted island.

Good confronts Evil when the Phantom seeks to rescue Diana while also stopping Drax and the Sengh Brotherhood from uniting the three skulls and becoming a powerful force in the world.

Phantom lore is fascinating, especially the idea that he never dies, or, at least, that's what criminals and evildoers everywhere think. The Ghost Who Walks has been around since 1936, which predates Superman, making the Phantom one of the earliest superheroes.

I remember seeing trailers for this flick back when it first came out and getting all excited. It was a superhero, swashbuckling adventure.

Even saw it in the theatre. On that day I was running a bit behind. If I remember right, I missed the previews and came in right when the movie was starting. The first words I saw were the words that kicked off the film, "For those who came in late." I really thought the movie somehow knew I was late—or people like me—because then it went into a recap of the Phantom's origin before launching into the main story. Ahh, to be a young, gullible fanboy again.

This movie was clean, wholesome superhero fun. There was a decent story, superhero action, humor and adventure, with a little romance thrown in. It didn't take itself seriously, but wasn't a giant camp-fest either. I still pop it in the DVD now and then and enjoy *The Phantom* as a nice break from the oh-so-heavy-drama-laden superhero movies of today. Sometimes you just want to see a good guy busting bad guys and that's it.

Nowadays, this movie falls short in a few places—the "wow factor," the costume, the life-or-death-save-the-world-or-die storylines—but I was happy with Billy Zane's portrayal of the Phantom and with the movie as a whole. I've never read any of the comics so my view is completely on the flick and it being a simple superhero story. I will say that this movie has stirred in me an interest in the Phantom and am thinking of one day getting into the comics that spawned him.

The movie is definitely kid-friendly and as a parent who doesn't let his kids watch a good chunk of today's superhero flicks due to their mature content, this is one I'd recommend for families or those just looking for a break from the more grownup, adult-oriented superhero movies of today.

Planet Hulk (2010)
Written by Greg Johnson
Directed by Sam Liu
Runtime 81 min.
3 out of 5

An ancient prophecy. An exiled hero. One battle after another.

Hulk has been banished into space by the Illuminati. The reason? He's simply too dangerous, too powerful and too unpredictable. Upon landing on the planet Sakaar, Hulk is taken captive and is forced to compete as a gladiator for the people's entertainment. With no choice but to fight, Hulk must battle his way free, and not only for himself, but for an entire kingdom under the rule of an unpleasant emperor. Is Hulk the one foretold to come to usher in an era of peace?

I don't know, man. This flick wasn't really my thing, to be honest. It was a kind of *Star Wars* meets superhero thing that, while kind of interesting, didn't really thrill me as a superhero fan.

But first, the pluses:

Loads of action. Hulk is fighting people pretty much all the time in this movie, and not only simply fighting them, but having to struggle against those nearly as powerful as himself. You don't often see him doing that.

The sci-fi aspect was different and by having the story not take place on Earth, you got to see something that isn't presented all too often in superhero flicks and/or cartoons.

The minuses (for me):

Hulk was the smart Hulk in this movie. Not the genius-level one, but he formed complete sentences, had genuine feelings, and wasn't a big ball of rage like in *Hulk vs.* I'm a fan of the latter. I like the Hulk-smash Hulk. Not quite stupid, but certainly simple-minded, and an all-out force of meta-nature. Seeing him pretty much be a big green human wasn't really my thing. I know others like that version of Hulk, which is fine, but I like the other one better.

The pacing was slow as well, with flashbacks that seemed to bog it down versus add to it. I know why they had them, but they didn't really add to the tale and those scenes could've been simply mentioned versus shown.

Art's subjective, but the cartooning style of this flick wasn't up my alley. Whatever. It's a minor point.

Wish I could say more about it, but this Hulk outing didn't grab me like *The Incredible Hulk* or *Hulk vs.*

However, if you're a Hulk fan, I'm sure you'll enjoy it for that reason, and if you like the more intelligent Hulk, you'll have a good time for sure.

The Punisher (2004)
Written by Jonathan Hensleigh and Michael France
Directed by Jonathan Hensleigh
Runtime 124 min.
4.5 out of 5

Frank Castle (Thomas Jane) has just completed his final mission with the FBI: posing as European arms dealer Otto Krieg to lure Bobby Saint—son of crime boss Howard Saint (John Travolta)—into a deal and eventually put him away. A shootout ensues and Bobby is killed. Frank retires and heads down to Florida on vacation with his family. When Howard Saint discovers Frank's true identity and that "Krieg" didn't die in the shootout, he sends a team of men to take out Frank's family as payback for killing his son. Howard Saint's men kill everyone including, they think, Frank. But Frank survives—barely—and soon gets well enough to punish Howard and his family slowly and painfully in an effort to balance the scales of justice.

I'm a huge fan of this movie despite there being a big divide amongst fans about it. Personally, it hit home to me on a lot of levels and this is why I love it. It's a story of tragedy and pain, things going south in a big way, and one man trying to make things right the only way he knows how. What especially impressed me was the overall feel of the film and how that reflected Frank's journey from family man to broken man to Punisher. In the beginning, everything is happy, cheery, colorful, and then once all are killed, suddenly the tone goes bleak, it's all grays and browns and blacks, and everything becomes ultra serious. Even the humorous bits are done in a serious manner.

I also liked the glimpses into the lives of the others in Frank's apartment building: Joan (Rebecca Romijn), Bumpo (John Pinette) and Spacker Dave (Ben Foster). To be honest, I don't know how true they were to their comic book counterparts as I haven't read them, but as portrayed on film, I liked them as characters and had a soft spot for each of them as I saw bits and pieces of others I once knew inside them.

Back to Frank, Thomas Jane played it in spades. He was depressed, brooding, angry, idealistic, righteous and distraught all at the same time.

He brought each of these elements to the fore whenever they were best called upon and went beyond just a gun-wielding vigilante. He would've made an excellent Batman should he have ever been offered the role.

When I saw him as the Punisher again in the fan film, *Dirty Laundry*, I cheered him on the whole way through and felt like I was back at home in Frank Castle's life, walking with him as he dealt with the pain of losing everyone he'd ever loved while once again rising to the call of duty because he was needed.

Frank's inspiring speech in *The Punisher* about sometimes the law being inadequate gets every fanboy pumped up and cheering, and while I find it hard to believe Frank's motive is only punishment and not vengeance, it's still a memorable moment in the film.

This flick is one of my favorites and is highly recommended.

The Rocketeer (1991)
Written by Danny Bilson and Paul De Meo
Directed by Joe Johnston
Runtime 108 min.
4 out of 5

When Cliff Secord stumbles upon a rocket pack stashed away in an airplane, him and his friend Peevy soon find themselves on the run from gangsters with ties to the Nazis.

I saw this back when I was a kid and it's still one of my favorite superhero flicks, namely because it's historical, has a very human superhero, and is about flying. I mean, who doesn't want to fly? Better, who doesn't want to think they can somehow piece together a rocket pack, strap it on and take to the sky?

What makes this superhero movie different is it's not about a guy going around and helping people while trying to juggle a secret identity and, later, ultimately facing off against a supervillain. Instead, it's about someone who has something the bad guys want and spends all his time running from them, occasionally helping people along the way. So while true the standard superhero "ingredients" are there, they're presented outside of the standard formula thus setting this flick apart. Couple that with it taking place in the past during a simpler time—a classier time, too—and you've got a memorable movie.

I like how they also blended real life history into this, namely bringing in Howard Hughes as the designer of the rocket pack. Very cool. Throw in a Nazi as a main villain and you've got some solid Good vs Evil going on. Speaking of which, Timothy Dalton as Neville Sinclair the Nazi was awesome. He was super evil in this and once you found out who he really was you just hated the guy. You gotta love villains you can hate and feel justified in doing so.

There was certainly a pulpy feel to this movie, which is good, as the Rocketeer is an old time hero, a pulp hero, in fact. They kept that element alive, even so far as having him go up against a giant goon with a unique visage. Reminded me of the Dick Tracy villains. Sweet.

If you dig pulp heroes, *The Rocketeer* is definitely recommended viewing. Go see for yourself.

The Shadow (1994)
Written by David Koepp
Directed by Russell Mulcahy
Runtime 108 min.
3.5 out of 5

An avenging force for good and a terror of the criminal underworld, the Shadow operates in New York after dark, but when Shiwan Khan—last descendent of Genghis Khan—comes to the city and plans on world domination, the Shadow must defend the Big Apple from him. When the Shadow refuses to join forces with Khan, the two battle it out with the fate of the city hanging in the balance.

This flick was my first exposure to the pulp superhero when I was younger. With loads of shadows, gothic ambience, an exciting soundtrack and a hero with the biggest cape I'd ever seen, the Shadow quickly became one of my favorites growing up. I mean, he was kind of like Batman, but had a superpower—he could get into your mind, control you, make you see things that weren't there and thus become a "shadow."

Alec Baldwin as Lamont Cranston totally worked. He had the cool rough voice, the playboy debonair down to a T, and had an air of mystery about him that suited the character well. Good stuff.

Action-wise, no complaints. Nothing over-the-top or extremely spectacular, but enough to get the job done. I will say those shots of the Shadow materializing and dematerializing out of view as he fights is especially cool and spooky. I mean, how do you fight what you can't see?

The plotline was well thought out, especially because you're dealing with a hero and villain with mental powers, which isn't always easy to show people. It all takes place in the head, after all, so depicting the manifestation of these mental powers was well done.

This movie really had that old radio drama feel to it, which I'm sure was something the filmmakers were going for as *The Shadow* used to be a radio drama back in the day.

Some recognizable names in this flick, too: Sir Ian McKellen, Peter Boyle, Tim Curry.

The Shadow is an excellent foray into the "realistic fantastic" and I'd recommend it to anyone looking for pulpy heroic goodness.

Sky High (2005)
Written by Paul Hernandez, Bob Schooley and Mark McCorkle
Directed by Mike Mitchell
Runtime 100 min.
4 out of 5

Will Stronghold's parents are the world's greatest superheroes—the Commander and Jetstream—and his folks are hoping that by him enlisting in the super high school, Sky High, he'll achieve his full potential and become a great hero himself. Unfortunately, Will doesn't have any superpowers and must try and make his way out from under his parents' super shadows and through the trials and tortures of a super high school. When one of the Commander's old enemies, Royal Pain, surfaces, Will must find it in himself to be the man he was destined to be, and not just become a hero, but a *super*hero.

Seriously, Kurt Russell as a superhero? Yes. That is a good idea and I'm dead serious. He's got the looks, the charm and the coolness factor to pull it off. Turning him into a Superman rip-off makes it even more perfect so I'm totally down with Kurt Russell as the Commander. Throw in Kelly Preston as his wife and fellow super crime fighter Jetstream and you've got a match made in super Heaven.

This movie is a love letter to the genre, featuring all the things that make superheroes great. As said, you got the Superman-type hero in the Commander, the beautiful heroine ala Wonder Woman in Jetstream, and loads of students at Sky High exhibiting all the classic powers throughout the movie, everything from flight to heat vision, to freezing people to superstrength, to shape shifting to superspeed—the list just keeps going. Tell the story from the point-of-view of the Commander and Jetstream's son, Will (Michael Angarano), and you have the excuse to be on the outside looking in while also taking part in the adventure yourself.

It's a simple story, but a good story and, as said, was a love letter to the genre and the tale used to share that letter with viewers was a good one to do it with.

I've also made it no secret in my other reviews that I'm a fan of superhero comedies. Usually, they're done pretty well and *Sky High* is no exception. By making these superhero comedies and pulling it off, it goes to show how versatile the superhero genre really is. People generally view superheroes as so one-dimensional—sometimes two-dimensional—and that's about it. Doing an assortment of super flicks breaks that perception and as a diehard fan of the genre, I'm happy these other variations on men and women in tights are created.

This movie has fantastic cameos by the likes of Lynda Carter (TV's Wonder Woman), Bruce Campbell (*Evil's Dead*'s Ash—who is kind of a superhero on his own, in a way; I mean, Ash has a chainsaw hand for crying out loud!)—Patrick Warburton as the voice of Royal Pain (Patrick was TV's the Tick) and a bunch of other familiar faces. Nice.

Sky High is complete family fun, kid-friendly and is highly recommended for those looking to expand their superhero-movies-I've-watched repertoire.

Go see it. Buy it, borrow it, rent it—just see it. It's good times.

Spawn (1997)
Written by Alan McElroy
Directed by Mark A.Z. Dippé
Runtime 96 min.
3 out of 5

Seasoned soldier Al Simmons is double-crossed by his boss, Jason Wynn, and is assassinated. Heading straight to Hell, Al cuts a deal with the devil and is sent back to Earth. The catch? It's five years later and his beloved wife Wanda is married to his best friend. Worse, Al's rethinking his vow to lead Hell's war against Heaven. Endowed with the powers of a hellspawn, he not only looks terrible but is hounded by a demented and demonic clown and finds himself at a crossroads as to what to do with these new abilities. Deciding to take his fate into his own hands, Al begins to mark out his own path as Spawn.

This movie is a CGI extravaganza unlike anything that had ever been seen in a superhero film at the time. Most of the effects are computer, and I mean com-put-er, but those were how effects looked back then so whatever.

That stuff aside, the movie's all right. They got Al's origin right, but really seemed to tame down the gruesome exploits of a hellspawn for mainstream audiences. Realistically, a true Spawn film would be rated R and loaded with language and so much gore that even the most desensitized audiences would cringe.

Michael Jai White as Spawn worked for me. He was tough, brooding, had the grumbly voice, and the dude knows how to fight! (He's a real-life martial artist in several disciplines.)

John Leguizamo as the Clown/Violator was awesome. He was disgusting, funny, rude and was a thorn in Al's side right from the get-go.

The story seemed more like an overview versus the thick of Spawn's mythos. Spawn does have a dense mythology with a lot of players and it's real hard to get all that into an hour-and-a-half movie. At the same time, they didn't have a choice but to go short and sweet because Spawn—back then and outside of the comic book universe—was completely unknown. Even now, unless you're a comic fan, not many people know who he is. Hard to convince a studio to green-light a long Spawn movie.

On the plus side, this flick is intensely atmospheric and harkens back to Tim Burton's Batman movies in a lot of ways. There is a sense of Spawn's world throughout the film and not just, "Oh, this is happening in that city down the block." Some of the fights were top notch, too, especially the Spawn vs Violator battle when the Clown first reveals his true form. This was new for comic book flicks at the time and should not go unappreciated.

Maybe Spawn'll get a second shot at the big screen? There have been rumors of that for years. You never know.

Spider-Man (2002)
Written by David Koepp
Directed by Sam Raimi
Runtime 121 min.
4 out of 5

This flick was decades in the making. So many legal setbacks forced Spider-Man to bounce from rights holder to rights holder before finally finding a place with Sony to deliver the goods.

The hype surrounding this movie was astounding. I remember getting my copy of the soundtrack before the movie came out, and not just that, but also a copy of the "Hero" single by Nickelback as well. Seeing Spidey swinging over a golden-bathed New York on its cover got me even more stoked for this film.

And so, opening night, I went with my dad to check the movie out, my heart pounding with excitement, the previews before the movie taking excruciatingly long.

Peter Parker (Tobey Maguire), geek extraordinaire, gets bitten by a radioactive "super spider" while on a class fieldtrip as he tries to get a picture for the school paper of next-door-neighbour-slash-love-of-his-life Mary Jane Watson (Kirsten Dunst). Following a bout of sickness, Peter wakes up the next morning no longer a skinny geek but instead buff and tough, wondering what happened to him. Adding to the weirdness, he's suddenly able to do things he wasn't able to do before: no need for glasses; lots of energy; fantastic agility; amazing strength; sticks to walls; shoots sticky white web-things out of his wrists; can sense bad things before they happen. So, like any good teenager with superpowers, he uses them to impress the girl of his dreams, in his case, taking on a spider-like persona in a wrestling match to win some big money to buy a car. While on the way there, he fights with his uncle, Ben, and leaves in a huff, only to later find out the burglar he let get away—who had stolen from the wrestling folks who didn't pay Peter what he was worth—killed his uncle in an effort to swipe a getaway car.

Also going on, Norman Osborne (Willem Dafoe) is having trouble with his company and so, in a fit to prove to the military his superhuman formula works so he can sell it to them, he tries it on himself . . . but with dire side effects: the creation of an alternate personality which is eventually dubbed "the Green Goblin." When things go sour for the company, the board of directors votes him out and Norman goes into full villain mode to exact his revenge.

Across the city, Peter has learned that with great power comes great responsibility and so avenges his uncle's death by using his new spider-like powers for good and becomes the Amazing Spider-Man.

It's hero versus villain, Spider-Man versus the Green Goblin, in this superheroic slugfest/love story/coming-of-age movie that made the wait for this flick well worth it.

To be honest, however, the crazy overhype of this movie did put a damper on it for me when I first saw it. Straight up: when I left the theatre opening night I left disappointed. Not that I thought it was awful, not by any means, it was just there was this lingering "Is that it?" feeling that hung over me as I made my way back to the car.

If anything, *Spider-Man* is definitely an origin movie, something to set the stage for more to come, giving a rich backstory and atmosphere not just to Peter Parker's world, but to each of the supporting characters, even J. Jonah Jameson (who J.K. Simmons played brilliantly, by the way).

The effects were top notch save for a couple moments where you clearly saw that the Peter that was swinging and jumping from rooftop to rooftop was animated. Speaking of the swinging, when Spidey took you up and down through the deep concrete chasms of New York—man, you felt like you were there, swinging along with him. I heard they even developed a "spider-cam" for this movie. Cool. And that heartbreaking scene at the end where Peter turns down MJ? My heart bled for the guy.

Do I stand by *Spider-Man*? Absolutely. I saw it again in the theatre, going back with the mindset of "seeing it for what it was," and I adored it afterward. Out of the three movies in this series so far, it's my second favorite. As for my favorite-favorite, just read my reviews.

This was a superhero movie done right, done well and done just plain cool.

Recommended.

Spider-Man 2 (2004)
Written by Alvin Sargent
Directed by Sam Raimi
Runtime 127 min.
5 out of 5

Who ever said being a superhero would be easy?

In this second installment in the *Spider-Man* franchise, Peter Parker has his back against the wall as he tries to juggle life as a student, being best friends with Mary Jane Watson, carrying the guilt of his uncle's death, freelancing for the *Daily Bugle*, delivering pizza, and, of course, being ever on-call as your Friendly Neighbourhood Spider-Man.

No matter how hard he tries, Peter just can't seem to balance everything at once and the constant sacrifices he makes in his personal life so he can help others wears him down . . . down . . . down . . . until he can't take it anymore and his spider-powers begin to change.

Then vanish.

The timing couldn't have been worse, either, because Dr. Otto Octavius's energy device backfired and has fused four robotic arms to his body, their AI worming its way into his brain, controlling him. All they care about is fulfilling their purpose and they don't care who they have to hurt to recreate the device they were made for.

Dr. Octopus's (Doc Ock's) rampage through New York is met with little resistance until our favorite web-slinger attempts to take him on.

This movie thrills the inner fanboy much more than its predecessor and officially is my favorite—so far—in the *Spider-Man* series. This flick carries near start-to-finish classic superhero goodness: stellar aerial battles, eye-popping web-slinging, dual identity troubles, nerd-can't/won't-get-the-girl issues, a hardcore villain bent on his mark, trials, sacrifice—all crammed into a-little-over-two-hour movie. But the pacing works and doesn't feel over cluttered at all.

You feel for Peter Parker every minute of this film, both when he's at the top of his game and when he's at the bottom, and when he loses his spider-powers, your heart sinks and you cry out, "No! Not Peter! His powers are part of who he is. How can you take them away?"

Tobey Maguire was extremely believable in this film and brought a real depth to Parker that—though was present in the first one—really shone through in this. And Alfred Molina as Doc Ock? Such duality. When you first meet Otto Octavius, he genuinely seems like a nice guy, an almost fatherly figure in a way, but when he loses his project and those he cares about, things switch and he barely resembles the man he once was. Yet deep within, you see him struggling against the mechanical arms that have taken over his body and mind.

J.K. Simmons as J. Jonah Jameson was hilarious as always, and Kirsten Dunst as MJ—there was more maturity in the character this time around and though she still acted kind of "high school-ish," you also saw someone struggling with who they were—more specifically, trying desperately to reach out to the man she's fallen for but who is pushing her away.

Spider-Man 2 thrilled me to pieces. I was there on opening night and I left the theatre all smiles and in a state of disbelief at how downright cool it was. I wasn't sure if it would top the first one because most sequels— 'til that point because the Superman movies and the previous set of Batman films were pretty much what we had to go on except for *X2*— usually don't nail it like the first one.

I was proven wrong.

This movie rocked so hard I went back a couple more times and bought it on DVD as soon as I could.

Check this flick out. You're in for an amazingly cool, web-slinging good time.

Recommended.

Spider-Man 3 (2007)
Written by Sam Raimi, Ivan Raimi and Alvin Sargent
Directed by Sam Raimi
Runtime 139 min.
4 out of 5

It's triple trouble for Spider-Man in this third installment in the mega franchise.

Life is good for Peter Parker (Tobey Maguire). He's got the girl, about to propose, making bucks, the good people of New York love their Friendly Neighborhood Spider-Man like it's their job—yeah, everything is smooth sailing.

As if.

Suddenly, a mysterious new villain shows up out of nowhere: the New Goblin (though he doesn't refer to himself as such in the film). Quickly, we find out it's Harry Osborne (James Franco), Peter's once-best friend out for revenge because he thinks Peter murdered his dad.

One villain Peter can handle, especially since his first altercation with the suped-up Harry Osborne ends rather quickly. But no, things quickly get worse for our favorite wallcrawler when fugitive Flint Marko (Thomas Haden Church) gets himself trapped in a molecular blaster thingy and becomes the shape-shifting Sandman. Also adding to Peter's troubles is ultra-hungry photographer Eddie Brock (Topher Grace), who wants nothing more than to make a name for himself in the newspaper business.

Unbeknownst to Peter, while he and Mary Jane Watson (Kirsten Dunst) are on a date in a NY park, a mysterious meteor lands from the heavens, leaking a strange black goop that follows Peter home and eventually latches onto him, transforming him into someone darker, meaner and more spider-powered than ever before. When Peter finally realizes his new black suit is slowly destroying his life and he's alienating everyone he's ever cared about, he manages to ditch the suit in a cool church bell tower scene that screams Peter's search for redemption, but also Eddie Brock's search for revenge. The black goop lands on Brock, carrying a copy of Peter's spider-powers with it, transforming Eddie into the menacing Venom.

It's Black Spider-Man versus three villains in this web-slinging rollercoaster ride that scratches Spider-Man fans right where they itch!

The good:

The spider effects keep getting better with each installment, especially in the area of you feeling like you're right there with Spider-Man zipping through the air. That scene where Gwen Stacy (Bryce Dallas Howard) falls off that building and Spidey has to cut through the air in between falling debris to save her? Pure good.

The story had some good twists, especially building up the suspense while we waited for the black symbiote to latch itself onto Peter. Same with Peter proposing to MJ. The whole "it not working out" thing was well done.

James Franco played the villain wonderfully. I genuinely hated him after a while, the big tip of the hat being to when he fooled Peter into thinking he was his buddy again only to screw him over big time later on.

Topher Grace was easily the best actor in the film. He was funny, cocky, yet at times you sincerely felt bad for him.

The fight scenes were great. The symbiote effects for the living suit were fantastic, too.

The ending with Harry Osborne—even after all he did during the film—made tears prick the corners of my eyes.

The not-as-good:

One would think a major lesson had been learned from *Batman & Robin*: too many characters is just plain stupid. Unfortunately, *Spider-Man 3* didn't take that warning to heart. The film had way too much going on. I know they had to wrap up some story threads as established in the first two movies, but when all was said and done, things just felt way too rushed and I know I'm not the only fan to think so. If it were me, I would have left it at two villains: the New Goblin and Sandman. Or just do Venom and leave it alone. (And if anyone knows the Venom story, from the comics or the 1990s *Spider-Man* cartoon, you know that Venom's mythology is more than enough for a feature film.) I really felt short-changed regarding Venom. So much time was spent building up to him—the origin, Peter going dark, Eddie Brock's character, both before and after he inherits the suit—that by the time Venom showed up, there wasn't much time left in the movie for him to really be the bad guy fans know him to be.

There's really not much to complain about with this movie other than it feeling very rushed and cluttered. Over all, it still was a solid flick, but my least favorite of the three.

Rumor has it that *Spider-Man 4* is getting back to basics so I'm eagerly anticipating that one.

Also stars: J.K. Simmons, Bruce Campbell, Rosemary Harris, James Cromwell, Ted Raimi, Bill Nunn, Willem Dafoe, Dylan Baker, Stan Lee and others.

The Spirit (2008)
Written by Frank Miller
Directed by Frank Miller
Runtime 103 min.
3.5 out of 5

Denny Colt was one of the best cops Central City has ever known. After being killed in the line of duty, he returns from the grave as the Spirit and fights evil as a masked crime fighter. Enter the Octopus, an evil villain bent on gaining immortality and will do anything and stop at nothing to achieve it.

So basically this is *Sin City* meets an old pulp superhero, the Spirit, who was created by Will Eisner. We can thank Frank Miller for the *Sin City* spin on this flick as he was the man behind it. Which, to me, is fine. I thought *Sin City* was the breath of fresh air movies needed and adding that kind of style and storytelling to the world of the Spirit is cool with me. Granted, I never read the comics so I can't comment on if that was a smart move for an adaptation or not. I *can* comment that the costume change—going from an all-blue suit and fedora with a red tie, to an all-black suit and fedora with a red tie—was a cool move as a guy in a blue suit, a non-spandex one, wouldn't translate to film very well.

This movie is big time over-the-top, so leave your expectations for a realistic comic book movie at the door. The characters take a ton of abuse and keep on kicking. I mean, the Spirit taking a toilet to the head and still standing after? Come on. But if you go in not expecting a realistic superhero movie, then this won't bother you.

On a visual scale, this movie is aces. The black and white, the spot coloring, the glows, the different animated scenes thrown in—again, like *Sin City* but a really cool way to do a super flick and it makes me wonder how it might look if it was done with some of the more major franchises—i.e. if *Captain America* had a couple slick, three-or-four-second animated scenes as part of the movie. You never know.

Gabriel Macht did just fine as the Spirit—was tough, suave and able to hold his own on the action scale. Samuel L. Jackson as the Octopus— well, he's SLJ so you got SLJ. I love the guy but he's the same guy in every movie despite what he's supposed to be. Granted, there are a few exceptions (i.e. *The Caveman's Valentine*).

Bottom line: this is a crazy ride and cool detective story blended with superhero action and mayhem. It won't change your life, but it certainly might add to it in a little way.

Good movie.

Supergirl (1984)
Written by David Odell
Directed by Jeannot Szwarc
Runtime 125 min.
3.5 out of 5

After accidentally losing the Omegahedron, Argo City's power source, Kara Zor-El (Helen Slater) embarks on a journey to go recover it before Argo City perishes. Upon arriving on Earth, she discovers she has superpowers and adopts the identity of Supergirl, which she uses to help others while on her quest to recover the Omegahedron.

Elsewhere, the Omegahedron has fallen into the hands of Selena (Faye Dunaway), a flunky witch who quickly becomes powerful because of it and who sets her sights on Supergirl, ready to eliminate the Girl of Steel the first chance she can get.

Can Supergirl recover the Omegahedron before Argo City goes dark and Selena is victorious?

It's superheroine versus supervillainness in this '80s classic of Good vs Evil.

This flick is every bit a part of my childhood as the *Superman* movies were. At the time, of course, I was too young to understand the story, but now older, it's not too bad. Sure, it has some flaws and continuity issues, but at its heart it's the story about someone trying to right a grievous mistake, something that most of us can relate to.

The visuals and hints of Kryptonian mythology put forth quickly link it to the *Superman* movies—Supergirl identifies herself as Superman's cousin while in costume, and also as Clark Kent's cousin when she's in disguise as Linda Lee; her supersuit is basically the Christopher Reeve costume from the waist up—and it has a cinematic score that carries a similar heroic tone to that of its male counterpart. Likewise, Marc McClure reprises his role as Jimmy Olsen from the *Superman* movies and appears as Lucy Lane's boyfriend (Lucy is Lois Lane's younger sister).

They seem to want to jump right into Kara being Supergirl so don't give an explanation as to why she leaves Argo City in that bubble ship in one outfit then transforms inside the ship and flies out of the water in

144

her supersuit, but whatever. They do a good job of showing her discovering her powers, the joy of having them, and also the satisfaction of using them for good.

As hopeful and cheery as this flick is at times, it's also equally dark thanks to Selena being a witch. There is a ton of occult imagery and when you're watching this stuff as a kid, it creeps you right out. And that funhouse that Supergirl's "man in distress" has to find his way out of? Shivers, man. But who isn't afraid of creepy funhouses, right?

The pacing was pretty decent and each obstacle Supergirl must overcome as the movie rolls along keeps getting bigger and bigger until the end when it seems all hope is lost and even the Girl of Steel is helpless.

What was especially cool is during the time of Supergirl's tenure on Earth, Superman was elsewhere in the galaxy doing his thing, so when the story wraps up, Supergirl asks those who knew of her presence to forget she was there and flies off triumphant back to Argo City. This, of course, kept the two super franchises separate while still linking them. I heard Christopher Reeve was supposed to have a cameo in *Supergirl* but it didn't work out, with Reeve citing personal reasons (whatever those might've been). Would've been amazing had the two teamed up for it. Maybe we'll finally get to see Supergirl and Superman together in *Man of Steel 2* . . .

In the end, *Supergirl* is an overall enjoyable flick that is from a time before superhero movies got all dark and gritty, the hero was filled with angst and turmoil, and it enjoys itself for what it is: a movie about a girl who can fly.

Superhero Movie (2008)
Written by Craig Mazin
Directed by Craig Mazin
Runtime 85 min.
4 out of 5

After being bitten by a genetically-engineered super dragonfly, Rick Riker (Drake Bell) discovers he has superpowers and can stick to walls, has superstrength and can even fly! Trying to live up to the high expectations of the Riker family name, he becomes the Dragonfly, stopping evildoers wherever they may tread.

Meanwhile, evil billionaire industrialist Lou Landers (Christopher McDonald), trying to cure a disease that's killing him, tests an experimental procedure on himself. It goes wrong and he's left with the ability to suck the life energy out of people. For each person he kills, he can live an extra twenty-four hours. To accomplish this, he takes on the identity of the Hourglass and starts killing people left and right.

It's going to take a real hero to stop him and the Dragonfly is the right hero for the job!

This blatant superhero parody is basically a retelling of the 2002 *Spider-Man* movie, with a few references to other heroes thrown in (i.e. a scene from *Batman Begins*).

Part slapstick comedy, part tongue-in-cheek, part smart and witty, this flick travels in the vein of the *Scary Movie* franchise, the *Naked Gun* flicks, *Disaster Movie* and others. As a fan of all those movies, to see the superhero genre getting the same treatment made this flick even more of a delight. What makes these types of movies brilliant is the deadpan delivery of most of the lines, where every character plays both the straight man and the funny man, the roles interchanging between whoever they are playing along with.

Again, storywise, it's the *Spider-Man* 2002 movie, with names changed, a few different scenarios and, well, that's about it, so I don't need to recap here.

The action was fine, but obviously toned down because that's not what this movie was about.

Riffing on the *Spider-Man* 2002 costume, Dragonfly's suit was pretty slick, actually. Hourglass's, not so much.

The super effects were well done and believable, and it had a soundtrack that was a take-off of, again, the 2002 *Spider-Man* movie (I sense a theme).

As one who isn't a fan of over-the-top crude humor, I'm glad that that stuff was toned down for this flick. Maybe because they thought some parents would let their kids see it because it has a superhero in it, I don't know, but by doing that, it also forces the jokes and sight gags not to default to the easy stuff like sex humor.

Definitely a movie for grownups, *Superhero Movie* is a tip of the hat to the superhero genre from the comedy genre without it simply being a campy rendition of the same.

Funny stuff.

Superman (1978)
Written by Mario Puzo, David Newman, Leslie Newman and Robert Benton
Directed by Richard Donner
Runtime 143 min.
5 out of 5

Before the doomed planet Krypton explodes, Jor-El and wife Lara send their infant son, Kal-El, to Earth to save his life. Discovered in a field and raised by Jonathan and Martha Kent, Kal-El—renamed Clark—grows up to discover he has powers and abilities far beyond those of mortal men. After leaving the farm after high school, Clark heads north and meets a holographic projection of Jor-El and learns who he really is and what he is meant to do. Twelve years later, Clark re-enters the world and becomes Superman, a symbol of hope in a world that desperately needs it.

Upon observing Superman's debut, the greatest criminal mind of our time, Lex Luthor, hatches a clever real estate scheme to destroy the Man of Steel while also making himself filthy rich.

With millions of lives in the balance as well as his own, can Superman stop Lex and put an end to the madman's plan?

Like most kids, I watched this flick a thousand times. Okay, maybe not a thousand, but as often as I could considering my parents taped it for me and I knew how to work the VCR. At one point, I think we even had a VHS tape that had all four Superman movies on it from when they aired on TV. Anyway, I'll freely admit this review is totally biased as we're talking about a movie—especially a *Superman* movie—from my childhood, and it's impossible for me to watch the movie now without memories of being a kid, holding my Superman action figure and watching Superman catch Lois Lane falling from a helicopter that's stuck on the side of a building.

That said, this movie is still aces for loads of reasons. One, it was taken seriously. I read somewhere that Christopher Reeve—who plays Superman/Clark Kent—put forth that he wanted to do it straight-laced. Up until then, you had the *Batman* TV series for men in tights (unless you counted the *Green Hornet* TV series, which was semi-serious), and then the cartoons. There was the George Reeves *Adventures of Superman* series in the '50s and the Kirk Allen series before that, but in terms of immediate "superheroes in people" memory, you had '60s *Batman* and that was it.

By taking the source material seriously, by playing Superman as if it's really happening, this was the first time audiences were treated to superheroes in real life and the filmmakers weren't kidding when they said, "You'll believe a man can fly." I know I did, both now and when I was a kid. Superman was larger than life on the screen, whether he was using his powers or not. He inspired hope, and the film didn't shy away from showcasing a Superman that fought for "Truth, Justice and the American Way."

We got to see Superman enjoy being Superman, especially during his first night out saving a cat stuck in a tree, stopping *Air Force One* from falling to the ground, apprehending a jewel thief and putting an end to a criminal/police car chase.

Christopher Reeve as Superman has been the benchmark every other Superman actor has tried to reach. His Superman is bold, idealistic, hopeful and kind. As Clark Kent, mild mannered reporter for the *Daily Planet*, he did a fine job of really making you believe he was two different people when all he really had to use was a change of clothes, a new hairstyle and a pair of glasses. The guy changed his voice, his mannerisms, his speech—everything. I bought it. Go ahead. Put a picture of the two side-by-side and it's like two different guys, so I don't believe it when people nowadays say a pair of glasses is a stupid idea to conceal your identity. Ever have someone you know really well not recognize you after a haircut? It's happened to me and that's just a haircut not something covering part of my face like glasses. Anyway . . .

Margot Kidder was a solid Lois Lane: brash, driven and totally obsessed with Superman while being dismissive of Clark Kent. Her way of treating the two totally made the bizarre love triangle that is Superman/Lois/Clark work. Aside from some bad decisions that maybe we wouldn't expect a smart-as-a-whip reporter to make, she still sold it.

Gene Hackman as Lex Luthor. His version was good. I don't know much about the comics of the time, so I can't say how faithful he was. But in terms of being a good villain, for sure. And he was a bad guy here, an actual criminal and not the revered-but-shady businessman he would later become in the comics world.

The overall story: hey, it's simple, but so were most movies back then. At the same time, the superhero movies of today—as good as they are—could learn a lot from *Superman* and sometimes keeping things simple instead of just non-stop explosions and action is the better way to go. So much more room for character development and interaction.

This review wouldn't be complete without mentioning John Williams's iconic score. The "Theme from Superman" is right up there with Beethoven's Sixth. You play the tune anywhere and people recognize it. It's iconic, inspiring, heroic and like one of the folks who worked on the movie said—I think it was Richard Donner himself—you can actually hear the song say the word, "Superman."

Watch this movie. Just watch it.

You'll believe a man can fly.

Highly recommended.

Superman II (1980)
Written by Mario Puzo, David Newman and Leslie Newman
Directed by Richard Lester
Runtime 127 min.
4.5 out of 5

Superman is back, and when he inadvertently releases three inmates from the Phantom Zone, he has to go up against three supervillains every bit as powerful as he is. Complicating matters, Lois Lane is getting wise to the possibility that Clark Kent might not be who he claims to be and that, just maybe, beneath those glasses is the Man of Steel she so desperately loves.

As the two become close and spend time together, the three Kryptonian villains arrive on Earth and wreak havoc and destruction. Meanwhile, Lex Luthor seizes the opportunity to cash in on the aliens' arrival and tries to exploit their powers for his own gain.

With the fate of the world hanging in the balance and Superman nowhere to be found, will the Earth fall to General Zod forever?

This is a great follow up to *Superman I*, and is basically a direct continuation of that story, with seeds for this one planted in the first movie. This is also true behind-the-scenes as *Superman I* and *II* were shot simultaneously but due to various complications, the version that came out in 1980 wasn't completely what was intended, and thus the birth of *Superman II: The Richard Donner Cut*, which is the subject of another review.

Regardless, this version is fantastic, beginning with a recap of the Superman origin and mythology during the opening credits, and jumping right into Superman action pretty much from the start. The ante is upped by putting Superman against not only someone who is his equal power-wise, but *three* people who are, never mind Lex Luthor as well, who is a big challenge to Superman in the struggle of brains vs brawn.

This movie at its center carries a lot of heart as it goes into the relationship between Lois and Clark and Lois and Superman, making for a love story that is every bit as good as some romance movies without transforming this whole film into a romance flick. The ending is heart-wrenching as you understand the cost of being Superman and even the cost of being someone close to him.

Like its predecessor, Christopher Reeve and Margot Kidder know their roles and fulfill them to a T. Same with Gene Hackman. Obviously, a great deal of this has to do with them filming *Superman I* and *II* simultaneously, but in the interest of watching them from one movie to the next, that seamless transition adds to the believability of the whole thing.

Terrance Stamp stole the show as General Zod, easily holding up against Christopher Reeve and oftentimes overshadowing him. He carried with him a powerful presence, and gave off a rage that only one who had been—in his eyes—unrightfully imprisoned in the Phantom Zone could give. Sarah Douglas as Ursa and Jack O'Halloran as Non did just fine in their roles, but their main score was their reverence and allegiance to Zod, which then added to Stamp's performance.

The super battle at the end was great and awesome for its time. Most of the effects were practical effects—the best kind, in my opinion—and so while nowadays these guys wouldn't look so tough fighting it out on screen, back then I remember being in awe at how mean and powerful the bad guys were and how Superman really had a run for his money.

Superman II carries the same awe and wonder that *Superman I* did, even more so depending on what angle you want to tackle it from (i.e. *Superman II* showcases all of Superman's powers whereas the first one didn't).

Whether as a kid or an adult, I love this movie.
Recommended.

Superman II: The Richard Donner Cut (2006)
Written by Mario Puzo, David Newman and Leslie Newman
Directed by Richard Donner
Runtime 115 min.
5 out of 5

Superman is back, and when he inadvertently releases three inmates from the Phantom Zone, he has to go up against three supervillains every bit as powerful as he is. Complicating matters, Lois Lane is getting wise to the possibility that Clark Kent might not be who he claims to be and that, just maybe, beneath those glasses is the Man of Steel she so desperately loves.

As the two become close and spend time together, the three Kryptonian villains arrive on Earth and wreak havoc and destruction. Meanwhile, Lex Luthor seizes the opportunity to cash in on the aliens' arrival and tries to exploit their powers for his own gain.

With the fate of the world hanging in the balance and Superman nowhere to be found, will the Earth fall to General Zod forever?

This version of *Superman II*, the Richard Donner cut, was made possible by the outcry of fans. Eventually, the studio and Richard Donner—the director of *Superman I* and the original director of *Superman II*—responded and thus this version of the beloved super movie was born. Tracking down loads of old footage—most of which was shot when *Superman I* and *II* were filmed simultaneously, but then later discarded since with a change of director came a change in vision fans finally got *Superman II* as intended.

This version is way better, in my opinion. Better paced, better story—well, it's the same story but the "new" scenes are better and more well-written than the 1980 *Superman II* ones—and lots of heart and Superman fun.

For performance reviews, see my 1980 *Superman II* review as the actors did just as well in the alternate scenes shown in this flick.

While, yes, you can watch this movie after *Superman I*, you'll notice some overlap but don't let that distract you. When there was a change of director behind-the-scenes, it affected even the cut of *Superman I* that made it into theatres.

While attending a panel with Margot Kidder (Lois Lane) back in 2007, I asked her how this version of *Superman II* came about. Aside from giving a detailed backstory—however, I can't remember the specifics, it was so long ago—I do remember her saying that had it not been for the screen test footage that was used in the Lois-finds-out-Clark-is-Superman scene in the Niagara Falls hotel room, the one where she shoots him with a blank, the Richard Donner cut would've been released in theatres. I don't know if this is fact or wishful thinking on her part, but I know I would've paid to see this on the big screen. Easy. Obviously, the official Lois-finds-out-Clark-is-Superman scene in the Niagara Falls hotel room was never shot due to the change of directors and with Mr. Reeve's passing, it couldn't have been reshot anyway. I'm sure with Hollywood magic the reshoot could've been pulled off, had he been alive.

The big battle between Superman (Christopher Reeve) and General Zod (Terrance Stamp), Ursa (Sarah Douglas) and Non (Jack O'Halloran) is more exciting in this version, and likewise we find out what happened to the bad guys in this flick as opposed to them just dropping into a foggy chasm in the Fortress in the 1980 film.

The Lois and Clark relationship is better portrayed in this one, too, and that new scene with Lois trying to make Clark reveal himself as Superman when she jumps out of the Daily Planet window is more exciting than the "I'm going to drown myself in a river" bit that was in the 1980 flick.

There is also plenty of Jor-El (Marlon Brando) and Superman/Clark interaction, stuff that wasn't in the 1980 movie. It totally adds to the mythology and the overall sense of awe and wonder that is Superman.

For the Superman completist, this movie is a must-watch and a must-own. I know, for me, when I go to watch the *Superman* movies, I watch *Superman I* then *Superman II: The Richard Donner Cut*. I feel I'm getting the original story this way as the original script was so massive it had to become two movies.

Watch this movie. It's awesome.

Superman III (1983)
Written by David Newman and Leslie Newman
Directed by Richard Lester
Runtime 125 min.
3.5 out of 5

Gus Gorman (Richard Pryor) can't get a break, so he decides to go back to school and become a computer programmer. Finding out he has a genius-like knack for telling computers what to do, he quickly tries to make himself rich by doing so. After getting caught, the business tycoon he tried to rip off hires Gus to use computers to make him rich, namely by building a machine that can control the weather and cause different natural disasters which would in turn benefit the company. The plans are foiled when Superman (Christopher Reeve) steps in and saves the day. Now with the Man of Steel in their sights, Webster uses Gus's computer know-how to take down the Last Son of Krypton once and for all by synthesizing the one thing that can hurt him: Kryptonite.

Except, because of a slight alteration to the formula, Gus and Webster get something else: a changed Superman, one bent on evil instead of good.

Can the Man of Steel be restored before Webster has taken over the globe?

What can I say about this movie? It's a hard movie to judge because it was such a drastic shift in tone from the previous Superman flicks that on the one hand, you look at it as a continuation of the others—and it fails miserably—but on the other, you see it for what it is and it's pretty good.

Let me explain.

As strictly a superhero movie, it's silly. It was written as a comedy—probably to make Richard Pryor shine, who was a massive comedic star in the '80s—and that's where its downfall was. While Christopher Reeve played Superman straight like he always does, it didn't really mesh with the rest of the movie and as a result it's hard to take it seriously.

However, Mr. Reeve is stacked as Superman in this flick. Physique-wise, he totally peaked with *Superman III* and was even more powerful-looking than in the other films. I wish this presentation of Superman muscle-wise was in all of them. The super feats are great, you cheer him on, and your inner fanboy squeals with glee every time.

Storywise, some might call it silly. I call it: okay for the time. In general, the idea of a computer genius trying to take out the Man of Steel is a fine idea. Put him up against some tech-based problems and you could have a good movie. But this was the early 1980s and movie special effects were nowhere near what they are today and the budget wasn't there to put Superman up against some really strong computer-or-robot-based foe, so we settled for manufactured weather disasters and a super computer and woman-turned-robot at the end. Bummer. (But as a kid, the robo version of Vera (Annie Ross) scared me big time.)

From looking at it as a comedy, it's great. Pure gold. Richard Pryor wasn't called a comedic genius for nothing. Everything from his mannerisms to facial expressions to punch line delivery shines in this flick. The jokes are smart, sometimes slapstick and sometimes incredibly subtle, but always funny.

This movie would never go over well with audiences today and at a superficial glance, I can see why, but if you take the time to really look at it and appreciate it for what it is, it is a good movie.

Superman IV: The Quest for Peace (1987)
Written by Lawrence Konner and Mark Rosenthal
Directed by Sidney J. Furie
Runtime 134 min.
3 out of 5

The world is on the brink and Superman takes it upon himself to rid the planet of all nuclear weapons. Of course, war is big business and Lex Luthor sees an opportunity to use the Man of Steel's quest for peace as a way to make big bucks. By promising various war moguls that he'll destroy Superman for a cut of the profits, he puts a genetic stew made from Superman's own DNA aboard one of the rockets he knows Superman is going to throw into the sun. After the Man of Steel does, Nuclear Man is born, a being bent on the destruction of Superman and to do Lex Luthor's bidding.

Will Superman stand against this solar villain or will he fail and let the world fall along with him?

This was the last box office outing for the Man of Steel for almost twenty years. I remember my parents taking me to the theatre to see it when I was just six and a half. At the time, sure, I loved it. It was Superman, it was at the movies, and I had no clue what the story was about. Just Superman fighting bad guys and that was all that mattered.

Nowadays . . .

As a general premise, it's a basic idea: save the world, your main villain doesn't want you to and thus creates something powerful to defeat you.

But something gets lost in translation and there are so many laughable moments in the movie that it's the worst of the *Superman* movies when it could have been the flick to redeem the franchise after the misfire that was *Superman III*.

The special effects are terrible. I don't understand how the SFX from the movies nine years earlier were better. Most of the flying scenes were like a cut-out of Superman against a still back drop. Even in one of them, when he's flying along the river, you can see the wake of the boat from the camera crew.

The fight choreography was overly-dramatic and something you'd see in a school play.

It seemed they either tried too hard with this movie and it all fell apart, or they just didn't try at all.

As always, Christopher Reeve was amazing as Superman. That's who he was.

Margot Kidder was back as Lois Lane in this one and you can see glimpses of the connection she and Superman had in *Superman I* and *II*, but nothing comes to fruition in this. Granted, this movie didn't have any romantic elements other than one scene where the two fly together, which was just repeated footage cut over a multitude of backgrounds. (They fly around the whole world in that sequence in record time, too.)

There is a lot wrong with this movie with plenty of story and continuity inconsistencies, never mind the introduction of new superpowers that are not in the comics or other films (i.e. Superman rebuilding the Great Wall of China just by looking it).

There were, however, some things right with the movie. One of my favorite parts is when Clark *and* Superman are invited up to Lacy Warfield's (Mariel Hemingway's) penthouse. Clark has to keep coming up with ways to disappear and become Superman and vice versa without tipping Lois and Lacy off that the two are one and the same. This was well done and the ways he does it are very creative.

Gene Hackman's Lex Luthor—yes, he is the greatest criminal mind of our time and for good reason. He does the part just as well as he did back in *Superman I* and *II*. Who else would come up with a way to destroy Superman that would also make him stinking rich in the meantime?

This is one of those movies that if you go in and see it for what it is, you'll be fine with it. Won't change your life, but you'll be fine with it. If you go in expecting a stellar superhero movie, especially one that could stand toe-to-toe with the super flicks of today, then you'll want to look elsewhere.

Superman/Batman: Apocalypse (2010)
Written by Tab Murphy
Directed by Lauren Montgomery
Runtime 78 min.
4.5 out of 5

A spaceship lands in Gotham Harbor. A young woman emerges with powers just like Superman.

Welcome to Earth, Supergirl.

Upon learning of Kara Zor-El's (Supergirl's) arrival, Darkseid orders her capture . . . and succeeds. If he can control her, he can use her to lead the Female Furries army.

Superman, Batman and Wonder Woman track Kara down with the help of Barda, the old leader of the Female Furries, and take the battle to Apokolips to save Kara and stop Darkseid from going through with his plans.

Talk about raising the bar and setting the stakes so high that it takes the combined forces of Superman, Batman and Wonder Woman to save the day. Add the threat of an unstable and brainwashed Kryptonian by way of Supergirl and the all-powerful Darkseid, and you have a recipe for a strong superhero story.

The spotlight was on Superman in this one and that pleases this Superman fan. By introducing Kara into the mix, we get to see him come to the realization that he's not Krypton's sole survivor and that he actually has family, a blood relative (Kara is Superman's cousin; her father and his were brothers). To see him try and show her the ways of Earth, help her fit in the same way his own earthly parents aided him, is a definite passing of the torch. It also gives him a chance to explain why he does things the way he does.

Tim Daly returns as the voice of Superman in this. I love his voice for the character. He was the man on *Superman: The Animated Series* and every time I see his name in the credits of a DCU movie, I know I'll be happy with the Superman in the flick.

Kevin Conroy is Batman. No, I mean, he *is* Batman. He cemented himself as such in *Batman: The Animated Series* and continues doing so with every outing.

Summer Glau picked up the reins as Supergirl in this and sold the dialogue very well.

Darkseid—Andre Braugher—was okay, but I wish he had more of a commanding voice presence instead of just a deep one.

This movie is Supergirl's movie, to be sure. It was based off the graphic novel *Superman/Batman: Supergirl* by Jeph Loeb and the late Michael Turner. Not sure why they changed the title for this movie. Whatever. They also translated Mr. Turner's art very well to the screen. I love his artwork so was happy to see it animated as it was. He draws such amazingly beautiful women.

DC animated movies are good for including some fantastic extras and this one includes a Green Arrow animated short. It is pure gold and while I know the character is busy with his own TV show at the moment—*Arrow*—I hope DC at some point makes a full-length live action movie or animated feature with him. If this short proves anything, it's that they can do it and do it well.

Superman/Batman: Apocalypse is the total package and one I really liked a lot. Recommended.

Superman/Batman: Public Enemies (2009)
Written by Stan Berkowitz
Directed by Sam Liu
Runtime 67 min.
4.5 out of 5

The Man of Steel has been framed for the murder of Metallo.

Now on the public's radar as a wanted man, Superman must team up with his greatest ally—and closest friend—Batman, to clear his name and show the public what really happened the night Metallo died. But before he can do that, he must survive an onslaught of superheroes and supervillains alike, all of whom have come to cash in on the bounty for his capture.

Meanwhile, a giant kryptonite meteor is on a collision course for Earth, making things even worse for the Man of Steel who has no way to stop it, especially since the President of the United States, Lex Luthor, wants to destroy it himself with nuclear missiles.

Will the Earth survive and will Superman restore his good name?

This movie, based on the graphic novel by Jeph Loeb and Ed McGuinness, *Superman/Batman: Public Enemies,* is a comic book fan's dream come true. Not only does it feature all of comicdom's two most popular icons, but also a super supporting cast consisting of Power Girl, Captain Atom, Major Force, Black Lightning, Starfire, Katana and a host of other familiar faces, including, but not limited to, Captain Cold, Mr. Freeze, Bane, Lady Shiva and a ton of others.

The story is solid, simple, but enough to really showcase each character: Superman as the one who doesn't kill; Batman as the disgruntled detective; Lex Luthor as the glory-seeking, power-mad President—it totally works. The pacing was bang on and not once was I bored. Even the humor was in-step with the rest of the movie and didn't come across like jokes from left field. Case in point, the giant robot in the end would've come across as goofy had not an explanation been given for the way it looked.

There was a good give-and-take between Batman and Superman in this flick, too, both in their banter with one another, their approach to doing things, and also in saving each other's bacon. Sometimes it seems that whenever the two team up, it's always Batman that saves Superman. It was awesome a balance was finally struck between who helps who and when.

I'm a huge fan of Ed McGuinness's rendition of Superman and to see that they mimicked that art style in this feature made this fanboy happy. His Superman is big and strong and powerful. His Batman is top notch, too, same with the other characters.

Of course, having Superman voiced by Tim Daly and Batman voiced by Kevin Conroy only adds to it as these guys were the voice talent behind these characters on their respective animated series. I really wish they would've been used for all the animated movies, but sadly that's not the case and, of course, there're different behind-the-scenes reasons as to why that is. Regardless, each actor captures each character perfectly, their tone, inflections and presentation reflecting the hero they're supposed to portray.

Superman/Batman: Public Enemies was one of the early feature-length DC animated movies and still holds up to this day as a classic.

Highly Recommended.

Superman: Brainiac Attacks (2006)
Written by Duane Capizzi
Directed by Curt Geda
Runtime 75 min.
3.5 out of 5

When Lex Luthor proposes an alliance with Brainiac to take down the Man of Steel, Superman must pull out all the stops to stop the seemingly unstoppable Kryptonian cybervillain. Meanwhile, Clark Kent examines his relationship with Lois Lane and considers telling her who he really is, but after she is poisoned, the clock starts ticking as Superman must try to find a cure while also stopping Brainiac and Luthor.

I love the animated style developed by Bruce Timm. It worked wonders on *Batman: The Animated Series* and then later they did *Superman: The Animated Series* the same way, and then after that they did *Justice League* and *Justice League: Unlimited*. It's a great style and this flick was done in that style.

This movie was pretty good. Wasn't awesome, wasn't terrible, was just above down the middle, I'd say. Brainiac is a cool villain, a very powerful one because he's nearly unstoppable. Throw in some Lex Luthor action and have them go up against the Man of Steel and you know Superman is in trouble.

Everyone was who they were supposed to be in this, except Lex Luthor. He wasn't as dark and serious as he was in the animated series and acted out of character. That's too bad because Luthor is a big part of Superman's world so you want to get him right.

Tim Daly—I love that guy as Superman. He has the right voice, the right delivery and every time DC does an animated movie and he's voicing Superman, it makes those movies all the better as a result. Too bad he's retired as of this review and his son, Sam, has taken over. Maybe he'll come back one day.

I won't spoil it, but it did have a satisfying ending and, since this was Superman's last solo animated adventure in the *Superman: The Animated Series* universe, it brought a smile to my face. I won't spoil it here. You'll have to see it for yourself.

Containing all the elements that make Superman such a beloved character—the Lois-Clark-Superman triangle, Lex Luthor, the Fortress of Solitude, Perry White and the Daily Planet, even Metropolis—*Superman: Brainiac Attacks* is a fun movie, kid-friendly and is a great addition to any Superman fan's movie shelf.

Superman: Doomsday (2007)
Written by Duane Capizzi
Directed by Bruce Timm, Lauren Montgomery and Brandon Vietti
Runtime 78 min.
4 out of 5

Digging deep beneath the planet's surface, Lexcorp accidentally unearths the merciless killing machine known as Doomsday. Immediately, the behemoth of rage goes on a rampage, destroying everything in its path, and all efforts to stop it fail.

The Man of Steel, learning of the destruction and deaths in Metropolis, takes it upon himself to bring the monster down before more lives are lost.

The battle is epic.

The action is huge.

The consequences are dire.

Superman fails, falls . . .

Dies.

Adapted from the biggest and most shocking comic book story of all time, *Superman: Doomsday* is the emotional and action-packed tale of the life, death and return of the world's greatest superhero.

This story is dark, and not just because Superman dies. This isn't a kids cartoon. The themes are mature (i.e. Lois half-naked in the Fortress of Solitude), Lex Luthor, distraught over Superman's absence in his own weird way, is the most evil Lex ever seen in a cartoon and the things he does at some points in the film make you go, "Man, that's evil. Not just evil. *Hugely* evil."

What was most astonishing was the swearing. I never would have expected that from a Superman cartoon.

On the plus side, the battle between Superman and Doomsday is the greatest slugfest this reviewer has ever seen in a superhero cartoon (and I've seen nearly all of them). The story is solid and packs a lot in given the amount of time Warner Brothers seems to allow for these direct-to-DVD animated movies of theirs.

The animation is dynamic, the coloring bold, the art in the style of the *Justice League* cartoons.

This DVD includes a few special features, most notably the enthralling documentary on the life, death and return of Superman, chronicling the death saga from conception to fruition, with interviews with the many artists, writers and editors on the project.

A very awesome movie.

Superman Returns (2006)
Written by Michael Dougherty and Dan Harris
Directed by Bryan Singer
Runtime 154 min.
3 out of 5

The Man of Steel had vanished for five long years.

The world moved on.

So did the one person everyone thought never would: Lois Lane. She even wrote about it in a Pulitzer Prize-winning article entitled, "Why the World Doesn't Need Superman."

But that's not all that changed. Lex Luthor had swindled his way out of a double life-sentence with a new plan: create his own continent and wipe out all the others.

He just wasn't prepared for one thing—Superman returns.

It'd been almost twenty years between Superman movies when this one came out, the last being *Superman IV: The Quest for Peace*. Expectations were high, the hype was through the roof, a star director (Bryan Singer) was attached to it, huge names played some of the key roles . . .

The payoff: an embarrassing movie.

I remember feeling ashamed of my hero when I walked out of the theatre. Being a lifelong Superman fan, I thought *Superman Returns* would nail it and kick a certain red-and-blue wallcrawler off the box office charts.

I was wrong.

The story of *Superman Returns* is okay. It's nothing new, pretty much a rehash of *Superman: The Movie*, just updated with a different spin.

There are also several terrible and nonsensical moments in the film: Superman's son, Superman in the hospital, Superman lifting a massive island made of kryptonite and flying it into space even though just before that scene being around kryptonite made him virtually mortal.

It was tempting to give this movie two stars, but Brandon Routh's portrayal of the Man of Steel saved the day. He did a stellar job as both Clark *and* Superman. Aside from Christopher Reeve, he's my favorite boy in blue.

Kevin Spacey did an all right job as Lex Luthor—evil, funny, selfish, manipulative, king of understatement. But he wasn't evil-evil, unlike Michael Rosenbaum in *Smallville*. Though I realize they're different continuities/series, you'd think a grown-up Lex would be darker than his younger counterpart.

Warner Brothers et al. erred with this film because they didn't remember the secret to Superman: people don't want to relate to him. He's an icon, an ideal. He's not Spider-Man. We want to be amazed, put in a state of awe. People only want to relate to Clark Kent, not his cape-wearing alter ego. They blurred the line between the two when it should have been crisp and clear, and that is where this movie failed.

Hopefully the sequel will not be a drama, but a serious yet fun superhero movie, one filled with wonder, eye-popping action and a story worthy of the Man of Steel. I just hope they don't use kryptonite as a weapon against Superman. If they do, they're going to have to use a whole planet's worth to make a dent seeing as how a kryptonite island didn't stop him.

Superman: Unbound (2013)
Written by Bob Goodman
Directed by James Tucker
Runtime 75 min.
4 out of 5

When Brainiac shows up and threatens to destroy Metropolis, Superman and his cousin Supergirl must rise to the occasion and put an end to a foe that has deep ties to Krypton.

This was a good flick. Hey, it's Superman and lately DC's been pulling out all the stops and every time Supes gets the DVD treatment it's done really well. Supergirl's presence added a new dimension to the Man of Steel's animated movie exploits. Giving a quick showcase of her past, what happened to Kandor, and how those events created the motivations behind the Supergirl of this movie proved that sometimes less is more. Also understanding where she was coming from gave Superman a glimpse into a part of himself that he wasn't really ready to face: the need to sometimes go hard on bad guys for the greater good. Yet, being true to who he was, he was also able to soften Supergirl around the edges, which just goes to show how much you can learn from family.

The animation was smooth, the colors were clear, the action was great and the art was fantastic. The slightly too-long-of-a-face aside, I like the way Superman looked in this. The Clark Kent was so-so. More of a fan of the thick glasses than the more stylish ones, but whatever. In the animated series he had two thin circles for frames and that was it.

Lois looked good, too. My only gripe is, while I understand these movies are being made more and more for adults, there are parents out there who buy these flicks for their kids because a) they're superheroes, b) it's cartoons, and having Lois giving Brainiac the finger wasn't cool. Though I doubt it'll ever happen, there should be some sort of bold labeling or disclaimer on the package aside from the MPAA rating that lets parents know if there's content inside that is inappropriate for kids. This "giving the finger" is why I won't let my kids see this movie now. Something for DC to think about.

As a Superman fan, I've been loving all this attention the Man of Steel has been getting lately and since Batman was the focus of so many shows and animated features, giving the Last Son of Krypton a shot and a large amount of screen time helps balance all that out. I also hope DC has plans in the works for other animated movies for other characters, JLA stuff aside.

What can I say? DC and Warner Bros. keep knocking these flicks out of the park. Now, if they translate this awesome sensibility and sensitivity to the comics to the big screen on a consistent basis, then superhero fans will truly be living in a new golden era of superhero cinema.

Superman vs the Elite (2012)
Written by Joe Kelly
Directed by Michael Chang
Runtime 74 min.
4 out of 5

Upon meeting the Elite, Superman hopes to have found new allies in his quest against evil, but when he discovers they bring a new brand of justice to the table, he must make a stand against them.

That's basically the premise of the movie and it's not so much a story with the fate of the planet hanging in the balance, but rather a story about the fate of how villains should be dealt with hanging in the balance. Bottom line is the question: is the world ready to move on from using temporal solutions to stop criminals—super or otherwise—to permanently stopping them by simply killing them?

Superman believes in the potential good in everyone whereas the Elite, led by Manchester Black, believes that if you mess up, you should die to a) bring justice to whatever crime you did, and, b) stop any future chance of it happening again. While in a way you can see where he's coming from, his black-and-white view of how to deal with evil leaves a lot to be desired. If anything, his view mirrors Superman's in that justice must come to pass, but Superman also believes in mercy and forgiveness and the idea of learning one's lesson then trying to make a positive go at things versus getting one shot and if you blow it then that's it.

Part of this movie asks the question about Superman's place in our modern society and if his ideals and motives are still relevant. Face it, we live in a very cynical, hard-edged world where people would sooner see the worst in others—while missing the bad in themselves, of course— than acknowledge people's shortcoming(s) for what they are, try to fix the issue(s), forgive and move on. This is the product of a self-centered society—especially in the West—so self-centered that we won't even acknowledge we have this issue (or get mad when confronted with it), thus creating the need to produce movies like *Superman vs the Elite* as, it seems, there are only a few who want to bring it to light.

That's the deeper stuff. The lighter stuff is this movie has a fairly interesting story to bring the above to pass. I did find it slow in parts. The action sequences were pretty good, especially when Superman starts battling the Elite. I wasn't a fan of the art direction, though, and have seen better presentations of Superman and his supporting cast in other direct-to-video DC movies.

If it weren't for the strong themes of this movie, I would've given it a three, but because it's about something important, it gets bumped up a point.

I do recommend this movie if you're not sure if Superman is still relevant today or if you find him an unrelatable hero. This flick might change that for you. Take a look and decide for yourself.

Thor (2011)
Written by Ashley Edward Miller, Zack Stentz and Don Payne
Directed by Kenneth Branagh
Runtime 115 min.
5 out of 5

Long ago Odin (Anthony Hopkins) led Asgard to victory against the Jotunheim Frost Giants and captured the source of their power, the Casket of Ancient Warriors. Over a thousand years later, Odin is about to crown his son, Thor (Chris Hemsworth), as King of Asgard, but the coronation ceremony is interrupted when the Front Giants find a way into the weapons vault and try to steal back the Casket. Fortunately, it wasn't stolen as the giants fell before they could take it. Wanting to make an example of them, Thor and some of his loyal companions travel to Jotunheim against his father's wishes and start a war with the giants. Odin rescues them but not without grave consequences: upon returning to Asgard, Thor is banished to Earth for his actions, powerless and alone. Only his hammer, Mjolnir, is sent with him, but now with an enchantment that only the worthy can wield it—and Thor is not.

On Earth, Thor meets Jane Foster (Natalie Portman), an astrophysicist who was there along with her mentor, Dr. Erik Selvig, the night Thor came through the wormhole.

Meanwhile, Thor's brother, Loki (Tom Hiddleston), finds out that his own heritage is not what he was told and, upon finding out his true origin, seeks to ensure his brother never returns to Asgard so he could become the king instead.

While on Earth, Thor must learn what it means to be humble, care for others, and thus earn his place as the proper king of Asgard, all in time to stop his brother from leading the Frost Giants into Asgard and destroying Odin's kingdom.

This flick was Marvel's fourth film in its Phase One plan leading up to *The Avengers*.

I love this movie. It's down-to-earth, fun, has a good story and enough action to keep things exciting but not so much that it bogs down the entire movie.

Up until this flick, Thor was basically an unknown character to the movie-going public, and *Thor* does its job on giving the character a rich history, making you care about him, and making you cheer him on on his path to redemption.

The scenes on Asgard were breathtaking—heavenly, even—the size and scope of the city enough to inspire awe. The stuff on Earth, well, it's just the stuff on Earth and this is the first I've personally seen the realms of fantasy and reality merge so well. There was a bit of that in the *Harry Potter* movies, but those kids never went to another world where it's fantasy-type stuff 24/7.

The special effects were awesome and, to me, were a kind of unintentional preview to an exciting live action Superman movie, with Thor being the one in the red cape this time. The flying sequences were powerful, the strength, the lightning blasts—all good stuff, and with *The Avengers* on the horizon, the climatic fight scene between Thor and the Destroyer was well-paced and well done, saving Thor's best for the ensemble film to come a year later.

The relationship between Thor and Loki was done especially well because most siblings feel that their parents favor one above the other. There's always going to be some sibling rivalry, jealousy and competitiveness. This flick nailed that, in my opinion, especially on Loki's side of things. I mean, at times you can't help but feel bad for the guy and sympathize with his motives (that's the mark of a good villain, by the way).

Thor is a sweet introduction to the character, sets him up really well for *The Avengers,* and this reviewer can't wait to check out *Thor: The Dark World* and see how the Mighty Thor grows as a hero and as Asgard's king.

Ultimate Avengers: The Movie (2006)
Written by Greg Johnson
Directed by Curt Geda and Steven E. Gordon
Runtime 71 min.
4 out of 5

In World War II, the Nazis tried to launch an intercontinental missile and was thwarted by Captain America, but at great cost: Captain America fell into icy waters and was presumed dead. Some sixty years later, he was found and revived by S.H.I.E.L.D., who ends up convincing him to join their fight against the alien Chitauri. When the Chitauri attack, S.H.I.E.L.D. implements Project Avenger and begins assembling together Earth's Mightiest Heroes to take on the Chitauri and put a stop to them once and for all.

This ensemble flick is one of the greats and is a solid introduction for the uninitiated to the Avengers—Captain America, Iron Man, Thor, Black Widow, Giant Man, Wasp and Hulk—all led by Nick Fury.

It's evenly paced, exciting, and gives each member of the team enough screen time to give them a chance to lock in with the viewer and make that viewer-character connection before moving on to the next guy.

Marvel's direct-to-video efforts have been lacking and haven't been that great because they've been very busy—albeit very successfully—focusing their efforts on bringing their heroes to the big screen. *Ultimate Avengers* and its sequel are the major exceptions to their animated shortcomings and this movie is every bit as good as their live action counterparts. I also think that's the secret to making a good animated movie: treat it with the same care and seriousness as a live action film and you'll hit it out of the ballpark every time. It works in Japanese animation. No reason why it wouldn't work here in the West.

This movie was good start to finish. Had a story that spanned decades, and made you care about what was going on from first frame to last.

You have multiple plotlines going on, ranging from the Avengers dealing with the Chitauri to Bruce Banner trying to find a cure for the Hulk, to Captain America trying to find his place in the world. The amazing thing is they fit all these plotlines into a very short runtime (just over an hour).

The art direction was superb and I enjoyed how everyone looked in this, especially Hulk. (For me, he's one of those guys that don't always come out well.)

While there's a pretty good dose of violence in this movie, it's much more kid-friendly than the majority of DC's animated features and is safe for kids (depending on your household rules for this sort of thing). Personally, I let my kids watch it but don't let them watch the DC movies.

Whether a Marvel fan, an Avengers fan, or a superhero fan in general, *Ultimate Avengers* is a fantastic flick worth watching many times over. What's cool is it's basically part one of two and goes right into its sequel, *Ultimate Avengers 2: Rise of the Panther*, without missing a beat, so if you have both, you're in for a doubly-good time.

Recommended.

Ultimate Avengers 2: Rise of the Panther (2006)
Written by Greg Johnson
Directed by Will Meugniot and Richard Sebast
Runtime 73 min.
4 out of 5

Picking up pretty much right where *Ultimate Avengers* left off, *Ultimate Avengers 2* starts off in Wakanda and the kingdom falls under attack from Herr Kleiser, who kills the king and sends the prince, T'Challa, into action by taking up the mantle of the Black Panther. Black Panther then heads to the city to find Captain America. The Avengers are assembled and head to Wakanda to stop the Chitauri threat, resuming their battle from the first movie.

I liked the first movie a bit better, but probably because it was the birth of the Avengers vs them in full swing but that's just me: I like origin stuff. *Ultimate Avengers 2*, however, is still a solid flick and falls right in line with its predecessor. (Always recommend watching these two back-to-back if you have the time, and with a little-over-an-hour runtime each, that's definitely doable.)

The battles in this flick are awesome and showcase some all-out superhero-vs-alien mayhem. Like the first, each character gets their moment to shine and it's like being reacquainted with old friends.

I love the depiction of the Avengers in this. Everyone is their stereotypical selves, something that they captured in the live action movie, but, to me, got even more right in this flick. Totally adds to it.

Like the first, the art direction is top notch. Everyone matches the way they looked in the first movie, giving it that sense of continuity. They had the same voice talent as the first for this as well. I love it when animated flicks keep the cast consistent outing-to-outing.

Watching this flick along with the first makes it a good final act to a stellar movie, but can also stand just fine on its own.

Glad I have it as part of my superhero movie collection.

Recommended.

Unbreakable (2000)
Written by M. Night Shyamalan
Directed by M. Night Shyamalan
Runtime 106 min.
5 out of 5

Ordinary David Dunn (Bruce Willis) has a failing marriage, a son who needs him, and a job as a security guard. However, all that changes after a severe train wreck and he is the only survivor. Even more miraculous, he is completely unharmed. When confronted by a man named Elijah Price (Samuel L. Jackson), who suggests David is invulnerable, David shrugs it off but eventually begins to test himself and discovers that maybe he's not that ordinary after all and soon learns he can do things no other man can. At Elijah's insistence, David explores his abilities even more and soon begins a journey that reveals maybe he is indeed unbreakable.

I've said it before and I'll say it again: I love superhero origin stories and *Unbreakable* is just that. Written and directed by M. Night Shyamalan of *Sixth Sense* fame, *Unbreakable* is a story deconstructing the superhero, and suggesting a possible real life origin for these amazing people, while keeping your interest from start to finish.

Using the real-life medical condition osteogenesis imperfecta as a springboard, suggesting that if someone with such frail bones can exist, is it not possible someone with unbreakable bones—even body—can exist? And thus is the story as we follow Elijah Price as he searches out this amazing possibility in the person of David Dunn.

This movie also heavily references comic books, Elijah posing the idea that comic books are modern day retellings of stories of times past and of real people who once were able to do things other people couldn't.

Each moment of this movie is an in-depth look at what makes the superhero tick, everything from the discovery of his power, to his motivation in using it, to the doubt that such a possibility could exist in a person, to finding a possible weakness, to balancing having this special ability with the demands of everyday life, and more.

This movie is a drama and not an action flick. While there is some action, namely toward the end, it's a life and times superhero story that makes you stop and think about what being a person with an extraordinary ability might actually be like, if it would be easy or hard, or a bit of both. What kind of challenges would you face? What kinds of benefits?

Apparently, M. Night Shyamalan came up with the idea following the standard three-part structure of a superhero story: the origin, the rise to being a hero, then the final confrontation with the villain. The movie has all these elements, but because he found it the most interesting, Shyamalan spends most of the time focusing on the origin. As a result, there is such depth surrounding David Dunn and Elijah Price that as the hero and villain, they rival characters that have been around for decades in terms of richness. Very well done.

This movie is just so, so good and is one of my all-time favorites. It's one of those flicks to throw on on a rainy day, get under a blanket, and get swept up in the world of the superhero only to be inspired to look for the spectacular in one's own self.

Highly recommended.

V for Vendetta (2005)
Written by The Wachowski Brothers
Directed by James McTeigue
Runtime 132 min.
4.5 out of 5

In the late 2020s, the United Kingdom is the only last stable government in the world and is led by the oppressive Norsefire party. Under such a tight regime, the people are controlled at every turn. The exchange? Bow down and you'll live in peace and safety.

From out of the shadows rises V (Hugo Weaving), a Guy Fawkes-mask-wearing caped activist who has a thorough plan meant to topple the present government and, over the course of a year, expose the Norsefire regime for what they really are and inspire the people to be free.

After being saved by V from an attempted rape, Evey Hammond (Natalie Portman) goes into hiding in V's lair and learns not only of V's plans for the UK, but also about herself, her fears, and what it will take for her to rise from her own ashes to help him on his quest.

This movie was based on the graphic novel by Alan Moore and David Lloyd.

Hugo Weaving is insane in this. His acting is through the roof! I mean, come on, the guy had a mask on the entire time. You don't see his face, and yet with every nuance of every word, every expressive tone, every bit of body language, you didn't need the aid of a face to sell you on what he was saying or why he was saying it. No small feat and was truly amazing. And that "V speech" when he introduces himself to Evey? Go. Watch it. Now. Awesome.

Natalie Portman is the bomb as Evey Hammond. I love her in nearly everything she does and her performance in *V for Vendetta* is no exception, especially when her character starts going through the wringer and she starts to break down. That scene where she gets her head shaved? That happened in real life. That was really her hair and was a one-take deal shot with three cameras, and a very poignant scene in the film. Her journey from start to finish is the audience's on-screen link to

V and his quest, and by the end, you're with him one hundred percent.

While there are some differences between the movie and the graphic novel, they by no means take away from it, in my opinion. There will always be differences when adapting books to film.

V in this flick is a kind of Robin Hood-meets-Zorro figure, but instead of having the people behind him, he's on his own with only Evey at his side. However, over the course of the year the story takes place, and as V unfolds his plan, the people start to get behind him, first in their hearts and then in their actions.

Speaking of action, I love V's fighting in this, spinning his swords and holding his own against multiple opponents. Some of the trickery he uses to evade capture also reminds me of Batman-like tactics.

The movie is a strong one, interesting from start to finish, and one that not only inspires, but makes me grateful I live in a free country like Canada and not in a fascist state.

V for Vendetta also spilled over into the real world—our world— inspiring folks to wear Guy Fawkes masks during public demonstrations, like Occupy Wall Street. If that doesn't show the impact of a movie, I don't know what does.

This is a superhero movie with depth and is an important addition to any superhero fan's library.

Highly recommended.

Watchmen: Tales of the Black Freighter & Under the Hood
Written by Zack Snyder and Alex Tse
Directed by Daniel DelPurgatorio and Mike Smith
Runtime 26 min.
4 out of 5

The DVD contains two features: *Tales of the Black Freighter*, an animated adaptation of that oh-so-bloody pirate comic embedded in the overall *Watchmen* strip (by Alan Moore and Dave Gibbons), and *Under the Hood*, a TV show interview with Hollis Mason (Stephen McHattie) about his bestselling, tell-all autobiography regarding his time as the original Nite-Owl during the first superhero boom of the late '30s/early '40s.

Tales of the Black Freighter was remarkable, grisly, and just plain cool. Even if you don't like pirate stories, it's guaranteed you'll dig this. It's a story about survival, the need to save others and the consequences of choosing that path, and what might happen to a man who becomes so obsessed with an ideal that he runs the risk of distorting reality completely.

Under the Hood was equally well done. Done as a "look back" magazine television show—complete with commercial breaks using products from the *Watchmen* graphic novel—it explores the origin of the superhero fraternity through the very realistic eyes and humble spirit of Hollis Mason. You forget that it's fiction quite easily and the segment also has that nostalgic feel of the *Watchmen* movie.

Also included is the very cool motion comic of the first chapter of the *Watchmen* graphic novel. This was just plain cool and the animation was far more than I expected. Thought I was only going to get a few sliding frames ala some anime segments but instead got a lot of animation for each panel of the graphic novel. In fact, this segment alone sold me on getting the whole graphic novel animated DVD. Likewise, you also get a behind-the-scenes featurette on the back stories that are *Tales of the Black Freighter* and *Under the Hood* and what they mean to the overall *Watchmen* experience.

The reason I gave it four stars instead of five is *solely* because five stars means I've been blown away and, well, the *Watchmen* theatrical film already did that and this isn't quite as good. It's my hope, however, that on the *Watchmen* director's cut they splice in *Tales of the Black Freighter* as shown above. Very cool. They shot all the newsstand scenes with the kid reading the comic book for it anyway so might as well use them.

Recommended.

Watchmen: The Ultimate Cut (2009)
Written by David Hayter and Alex Tse
Directed by Zack Snyder
Runtime 215 min.
5 out of 5

After the Comedian has been murdered, lone remaining vigilante Rorschach begins an investigation into his old acquaintance's death. Since most superheroes were banned from existing after some legislation several years before, he looks up old allies and even old enemies in his quest for the truth. Slowly, he begins to unravel a plot that could bring about a disaster unlike anything the world has ever seen before.

Based on what some would argue is the greatest graphic novel and superhero story of all time, *Watchmen* written by Alan More and Dave Gibbons, this movie adaptation was years in the making. Not this specific rendition, but from what I know, the book was optioned way back when it came out in the '80s but never got off the ground. One of the reasons was very few filmmakers had the guts to touch it because *Watchmen* is such a revered work amongst comic fans and even in some literary and academic circles.

Enter director Zack Snyder (*Dawn of the Dead* (2004), *Man of Steel, 300* and more), whose eye for detail and a knack for visual storytelling takes on the gargantuan project and does his best to faithfully adapt *Watchmen* to the big screen. Him and his creative team nail it, in my opinion, and adapt the book the only way something like *Watchmen* could be adapted: panel-by-panel. It was the safest route but also the smartest. Some changes were made—like the ending—but for the most part, the book is translated completely as is to the big screen. Even the director's cut includes additional scenes and animated clips from *Tales of the Black Freighter* interspersed throughout just like the graphic novel has bits of the pirate comic peppered throughout the main narrative.

Watchmen asks the question: what would superheroes be like if they existed in the real world? Whether they are of the superpowerless variety or something more Superman-like ala Dr. Manhattan, you get an honest portrayal of superheroes in real life, all centered around the mystery of the murder of one of their friends.

This story is about as down-to-earth as you get regarding superheroes in real life, and depending on the angle you're coming from, can be equal to or more so than *Kick-Ass* in that regard.

Each character in the flick matched their character in the book, all the way from the crazy-yet-cynical Comedian (Jeffrey Dean Morgan), to black-and-white-justice-seeking Rorschach (Jackie Earle Haley), to idealistic-yet-obsessed Nite Owl (Patrick Wilson), to insecure-but-strong Silk Spectre II (Malin Akerman), to misguided-but-you-can-see-how-he's-right Ozymandias (Matthew Goode), and a supporting cast that makes every moment believable.

The *Watchmen* story is so dense that the fact they were able to take the twelve-part series and showcase nearly all of it in around three and a half hours—I'm talking about the ultimate cut of the movie, which includes *Tales of the Black Freighter* and a bunch of additional footage not seen in the theatrical release—is pretty impressive. What's amazing about the *Watchmen* narrative and thus the movie is the incredible amount of history for the characters that needed to be shown without bogging down the main story, which was the Comedian's murder. You get to know these characters intimately, their pasts, their present and in some cases, their future.

Zack Snyder's knack for visuals gave this flick its own flavor and tone thanks to the color filters on the film. The score is fantastic. The action scenes were well done and quickly-paced, using brutal fighting techniques and the right amount of blood.

Watchmen is certainly not your traditional superhero flick. It's a superhero drama and is meant for an audience who likes to have some thinking along with their superhero slugfests. As a comic book fan, I appreciated the movie's faithfulness to the graphic novel, the overall story of *Watchmen*, and how each person involved really seemed to take this movie seriously. Nothing was tongue-in-cheek.

Watchmen ranks right up there as one of the greatest superhero movies of all time. If you consider yourself a superhero fan, then you should check it out. It's a serious look at the genre through the lens of a clever story with amazing characters, all of which you feel like you've known for ages instead of just for a few hours on the screen.

Highly recommended. Not for kids.

The Wraith: Eyes of Judgment (2005)
Written by Stephen J. Semones and Frank Dirscherl
Directed by Stephen J. Semones
Runtime 50 min.
4 out of 5

I'll admit I'd been looking forward to this film for a long time and when I finally received a *rough cut* of the film in the mail from the film's director, Stephen J. Semones, I was pleasantly surprised by what I saw.

The Wraith: Eyes of Judgment is based on *The Wraith* comic series and novel created by Frank Dirscherl. It follows the story of Michael Reeve, an honest and dedicated cop who, through an encounter with The Wraith, finds himself adopting the crime fighter's identity, both as The Wraith and the hero's alter ego, billionaire Paul Sanderson.

The good:

This is the first longer-than-five-minutes independent superhero movie I've seen and I have to admit I was quite amazed, and pleased, with what I saw. There was an atmospheric sense to the film that made you believe, yes, you were in The Wraith's world and you truly felt his presence. There's a scene right at the opening that does that—an encounter between The Wraith and a robber—setting the tone for the rest of the film.

The special effects were great—the CGI backgrounds, the "eyes of judgment" glowing on The Wraith's chest, the sweeps of the city—and there's no complaint from this fanboy here.

The music was amazing. Then again, when getting Emmy-award winning composer Larry Groupé (*Apt Pupil*, *The Usual Suspects*, *The Cable Guy*) to do the music for your film, amazing is something of an understatement. The music was heroic, dark and, to a degree, sad. It really carried a sense of emotion, which helped move the story along. Speaking of music, "Home of Darkness," sung by Mandi Leigh during the credits, was extraordinary and I wish there was a soundtrack for the film available because of it.

The action and fighting were great and there were some really cool, super-realistic sequences where I jumped in my chair after each punch or kick. There was only one fight sequence that lasted just a few seconds that looked rehearsed.

The story was down-to-earth, human, realistic and didn't carry the sense of "there's no way this can happen" like some of the superhero stuff coming out of Hollywood. You honestly believe that this story could happen in real life, which to me is a huge plus as I often wonder if superheroes could ever truly exist off the comic book page.

Having read both the novel and the comic, the major props for the movie go to Stephen J. Semones for directing a flick that was 99% true to source material. Of course a few minor changes had to be made, but that's film for you. Staying true to the comic or book the story is based off of has been time and again the biggest concern of fans of whatever franchise they happen to love. I'm happy to say Stephen nailed it on this one.

The not-as-good:

The story ended too soon, in my opinion. It felt like it was the beginning of a movie and didn't carry a sense of closure that the story was over. All franchises have "origin films" (see *Fantastic Four* or *Spider-man* or *Batman Begins*) and they're meant to be open-ended, but this one was a bit too open-ended. Though it was intended to pave the way for any future films, I wish there was something a little more finite to the tale. I still wouldn't let this point hold you back from checking it out. If anything, I was really disappointed it ended so quickly.

The acting, on the whole, was not bad. I understand independent films cannot hire the likes of Tom Hanks or Helen Hunt, but there were a few points where I wondered if the actor was monotonously reading his/her lines versus really saying them with conviction.

All in all, I'd give this film 4 stars out of 5. I'm looking forward to the DVD and all the extra features (and believe me, there's a ton of them) come September. I'll be the first in line to get one. You should be there, too.

X2: X-Men United (2003)
Written by Michael Dougherty, Dan Harris and David Hayter
Directed by Bryan Singer
Runtime 133 min.
4.5 out of 5

The rumored war between mutants and humans begins to take shape after a mutant makes an attempt on the life of the President of the United States. Soon, the X-mansion is attacked by military forces led by a man with a hidden vendetta against them. While the X-Men band together to make a stand against those who would rather see them killed or controlled, many of them must also face the demons of their past for good or ill.

Meanwhile, Jean Grey's powers are acting up and she's losing control. The others take notice and try to help, but something else seems to be brewing deep within her.

I love this movie. It was my favorite superhero flick until *Spider-Man 2* came out. This movie picked up pretty much where the first *X-Men* left off, and delivered in spades everything that made the first X-movie so good: solid story, amazing acting, high stakes (even higher in this one), and a respect for the source material. Throw Brian Cox as the main bad guy—William Stryker—into the mix and you got a recipe for a great movie.

Once again told from Wolverine's (Hugh Jackman's) perspective, *X2* is the story about facing your past and not running from what you find there. We see this not only when looking into Wolverine's life, but that of Stryker's, Iceman's, Rogue's, and others. Like the first one, the theme of being-different-is-okay is prevalent, and comes more into play as the government exercises its power while it seeks to investigate what it doesn't understand.

The hard part about reviewing an X-Men movie is that everyone does so well in their roles, you can spend a thousand words talking about each. Space doesn't permit that here, but needless to say I can watch Sir Patrick Stewart's father-figure and leader role as Professor X all day. Couple that with Sir Ian McKellen's—Magneto's—diehard devotion to ensuring mutants are ready for the inevitable confrontation with humans and you can see how these two characters are really two sides of the same coin with both wanting the same goal: peace for mutants. Of course, their means of achieving that goal are completely different from one another.

There's a real sense of world-building in the X-Men universe, with each location and character fully developed, and as we visit them with each outing, it's like coming home to old friends.

This movie is more intense than the first because, like I said, the stakes are higher and all those at Xavier's School for Gifted Youngsters are in some real life-or-death danger.

I also appreciate how they showed that if certain people had these special mutant-enhanced abilities in real life how much of a danger they could be to themselves and to others. This is something not often seen in superhero flicks as the villains in here—even some of the heroes— seemed more misguided than simply evil for evil's sake. And that's the kind of world we live in, right? How often are those who do something wrong doing so out of misguided intentions? How many times do we do that ourselves?

I'm really glad they made this movie and made it so well that the franchise has kept going.

I'm proud to stand united with *X2: X-Men United.*

Recommended.

X-Men (2000)
Written by David Hayter
Directed by Bryan Singer
Runtime 104 min.
4 out of 5

A small percentage of the world's population has natural mutations in their genetic code, each manifesting themselves differently. For many, it leads to special talents and abilities, but such capabilities come at a high cost: ostracization from society. Two factions have risen: one which believes that these "mutants" and the rest of humanity can live peacefully side-by-side, and another which believes a war is coming between mutant and humankind, one in which only one side will prevail.

Welcome to the world of the X-Men.

This flick is considered by many to be the beginning of the modern day superhero film era. Yes, we had *Blade* before this, but *X-Men* really cracked the door open in terms of taking a well-known comic property and bringing it to the big screen. Not only that, but there is some serious acting firepower in this movie, namely actors who don't do garbage, so right there that says something. Sir Patrick Stewart as Professor X, Sir Ian McKellen as Magneto, Anna Paquin as Rogue—yeah, big deal stuff. Then you throw who was then an unknown into the role of Wolverine (Hugh Jackman) and you suddenly have a bunch of talented actors taking a serious stab at a story about mutants with superpowers.

Bryan Singer was known for *The Usual Suspects* before this flick, and with him at the helm, we got an X-flick that was serious, funny in the right parts, plausible and just plain cool.

They did right to take the most popular X-character—Wolverine— and tell the story primarily from his point-of-view. I mean, this role made Hugh Jackman's career and it's a role he's gone back to six times, not including the upcoming *X-Men: Days of Future Past* due in 2014.

While the all-black leather costumes weren't really my thing—I liked the more colorful ones from *X-Men: First Class* better, which were based off the classic comic book costumes—they brought a level of realism to the movie and prompted that joke later on when Wolverine complains about the uniforms and Cyclops says, "Well, what would you prefer? Yellow spandex?" At the same time, I'm also in the major minority of people who think that properly-armored and modernly-stylized colorful superhero costumes could work in a real world situation. There are guys going around in The Real Life Superhero Movement dressed as such and are helping police after all.

Anyway . . .

The trick with an ensemble movie is to give each character enough history and density to make them likeable and relatable from frame one. When you have only a couple hours to do that, you need to have a story that revolves around each of them so they could each have their moment in the sun long enough to get the audience involved with them. *X-Men* does this for the most part and it's no easy feat.

Of course, there is the metaphor of the evils of racism throughout the movie, and how all people are equal regardless of who they are, what they can do and what they look like. This theme is strangely overt yet subtle at the same time. Kind of depends what frame of mind you're in when watching it and your personal history and feelings on the topic.

This movie is an interesting, exciting, thoughtful and well-executed big screen adaptation of one of the biggest comic book franchises of all time. Did they nail it perfectly? No. Did they do a good job of taking the X-Men concept as a whole to the big screen? You betcha.

Recommended.

X-Men: First Class (2011)
Written by Ashley Edward Miller, Zack Stentz, Jane Goldman and Matthew Vaughn
Directed by Matthew Vaughn
Runtime 132 min.
4.5 out of 5

After writing a thesis on mutation, university student Charles Xavier is approached by the CIA for his expertise on the subject as they've been tracking the villain Sebastian Shaw, who keeps mutant company. Once convincing the CIA mutants exist, Charles begins to form a team of mutants to go up against Shaw before he can execute his plans to start a third World War.

Loaded with thrills, excitement, stunning SFX, fun cameos and a strong story, *X-Men: First Class* is an amazing prequel to the X-Men films that won't leave you disappointed.

X-Men: First Class is one of my favorites. It was also a good chance to kind of give the X-franchise a boost after *X-Men: The Last Stand*. What was cool about *First Class* is it takes place in the same universe on the same timeline and is indeed a true prequel to the X-franchise we all know and love. Yes, there are some continuity flaws, but overall the whole thing flows. Besides, any other bumps that need ironing out can always be fixed with the upcoming *X-Men: Days of Future Past* as, well, time travel fixes everything.

The two main characters in this are Wolverine and . . . wait, kidding, it's Professor X (James McAvoy) and Magneto (Michael Fassbender), and this story goes way back to when they first met and were even on the same team fighting for the same ideals. You got to see how that friendship was forged because their friends-yet-foes relationship was so prominent in the other movies that to make it the spotlight of this one was a smart move.

This is truly an origin tale as you got to see Mystique (Jennifer Lawrence) in her humble beginnings, Professor X all the way back to when he was twelve; they recreated the Nazi camp beginning from *X-Men* for Magneto's origin and then expanded on that—which kicked off the main plot of the movie in which Sebastian Shaw (Kevin Bacon) wants to use the mutants under his command to kick off World War III—and also how Hank McCoy (Nicholas Hault) becomes all blue and furry as Beast.

Like the other X-flicks, this movie is amazing at being an ensemble film where each character is given care, the right amount of time in the spotlight, each having unique relationships with the others, and who-does-what-and-why is clearly explained. As a storyteller myself, I find this kind of writing fascinating because it's easy to fall into the trap of just focusing on one or two people and that's it, the rest of the supporting cast being way too *supporting* and not enough of their own people. I think the secret was the X-Men—whether good guy or bad—were approached from the angle of family, the idea that as mutants their mutation was their common bond and it was all for one and one for all regardless of personalities or even if people got along or not. There's even a bond between the heroes and villains of this flick because of their mutation.

The SFX were out of sight. The flying sequences were thrilling, the teleportations were amazing, the nods to the other movies—complete with cameos so watch closely—totally added to the world-building of the X-universe. That and the attention to the source material—using the yellow costumes from the classic comics, for example—and the overall story make this an awesome X-Men movie.

Man, just writing this review makes me want to go watch it again.

Highly recommended.

X-Men: The Last Stand (2006)
Written by Simon Kinberg and Zak Penn
Directed by Brett Ratner
Runtime 104 min.
3.5 out of 5

When a cure is developed to rid mutants of their unusual abilities, the mutant community is torn in two, with some more than happy to get rid of what they view as a curse, while others are vehemently against it. Outraged at this development, Magneto makes war on the humans for trying to rid the world of mutantkind and the X-Men stand in the gap to stop him.

This movie has a lot going on and seems to serve as an ending to the previous two movies, bringing to fruition a major confrontation between the X-Men and the Brotherhood. These two teams, while having skirmished in the other movies, never had an all-out battle and this flick shows that. It also brings to pass a version of the Dark Phoenix storyline with Jean Grey returning from the dead as the Phoenix and working for the bad guys.

From an action standpoint, this movie has tons of it and it's really cool. Wolverine (Hugh Jackman) kicks butt as usual, while having the Juggernaut (Vinnie Jones) running around and smashing into things makes you cheer. Magneto (Sir Ian McKellen) ups the metal-controlling ante in this—I mean, lifting a bridge? Flipping semis? Awesome!—and even having Beast (Kelsey Grammer) beasting it up adds a level of excitement that makes this comic-book-come-to-life a thrill. And when Jean Grey lets loose and destroys her childhood home while a bunch of X-Men and Brotherhood folks are fighting inside it? That was some jaw-dropping stuff!

From a story standpoint, it kind of falters. In a general sense—the overall story, I mean—it's fine as is. That is, the "what it's about." The delivery, however, seems to suffer from the same thing *Spider-Man 3* did: too much going on and not enough time to tell it in. Had this third X-Men movie either been part one of two or even the first in a trilogy where the mutant cure is introduced, a war brews, there's a big battle, some people die, etc. then that would've been fine. But it didn't happen that way. I don't know if that's because of a change in hands of directors or what.

The other thing that I didn't like—but could've worked had the story justified it/been expanded into another movie or two—was everyone dying. We lost some major people in this movie and for seemingly no good reason. I have no trouble with killing off major characters. It can definitely add to the story . . . when done right. In this flick, there didn't seem any justification for it.

What's amazing is thanks to the upcoming *X-Men: Days of Future Past* in 2014, depending on how that plays out, there's a chance of undoing some of the stuff that fell short in this outing and bringing back some people from the dead. After all, isn't that what time travel's for?

In the meantime, yeah, if you want a fun superhero movie, I'd still recommend *X-Men: The Last Stand*.

X-Men Origins: Wolverine (2009)
Written by David Benioff and Skip Woods
Directed by Gavin Hood
Runtime 107 min.
3 out of 5

Little James was born in the 1800s and was always sick. His family background . . . well, he didn't have much of one, at least, one that cared. Except for his friend, Victor. One night, during a drunken upset with his later-to-be-found-out father, James learned he could produce bone claws from his hands and defended himself, killing his father.

That night, James and Victor were on the run, and promised to always stick together. The years go by and the two find a great outlet for their rage: war. Victor (Liev Schreiber) also has a special ability and he is more animal than man, with claws coming out of his fingers. The two are very similar and age very slowly. War after war goes by, and the two eventually end up working with a secret team run by William Stryker (Danny Huston). While on one mission, James—now calling himself Logan (Hugh Jackman)—feels Victor has gone too far in his attack on an innocent and walks out on the group.

Years later, the group's been disbanded and Stryker comes to warn Logan that Victor is behind the recent string of deaths of its former members. The only way Logan will be strong enough to fight the always-stronger Victor is to undergo a special experiment of Stryker's own design: graft the indestructible adamantium to his bones. Logan agrees.

But there's something Stryker hasn't told him about what's been going on and when Logan finds out, he's furious and wages an all-out one-man war against Stryker, Victor and anyone else who stands in his way.

On the action: cool fight scenes and neat concepts. However, it seemed to me Logan was a little too acrobatic and was able to survive way more and take way more pain than even a mutant with a healing ability could.

On the story: works for me, in that we knew Logan had a history going in. He was the star of the X-Men movies after all, and *X2* especially focused on Logan's origins as much as they were able to without detracting from the main story. I did like seeing what really went on and, more specifically, how Logan lost his memory. I was under the impression that he lost it because of the adamantium experiment and not after it. Doesn't matter, but I did feel for the guy when the love of his life wasn't all she was cracked up to be.

On Deadpool, because, you know, it has to be covered: the whole story involving the secret ops group Logan was a part of made for fun action. Deadpool's origin, hey, why not? To be honest, I don't know if they followed the comics or not because I'm more a DC guy than a Marvel one and don't know too much about Deadpool other than he's the "merc with a mouth." His transformation from normal-looking Wade Wilson (Ryan Reynolds) to disfigured Wade—good stuff.

Was this a perfect movie? No, unfortunately. It felt too cartoony as opposed to carrying with it the realistic tone the other X-movies had, namely the first two.

Will I see the sequel? Absolutely. I'm a saga guy so I want to see what happens next.

Check this film out if you're the superhero-movie-completist type like me.

Zoom (2006)
Written by Adam Rifkin and David Berenbaum
Directed by Peter Hewitt
Runtime 93 min.
3 out of 5

Captain Zoom used to be a great superhero and leader of the government-sponsored superteam, Team Zenith. When the government tried to enhance his powers and those of his brother, Concussion, something went terribly wrong and Concussion turned evil and killed his teammates. Zoom stopped him and after the explosion, Concussion was presumed dead and Zoom lost his powers. Thirty years later, the government tries to resurrect Team Zenith using new kids with superpowers and recruits the retired Captain Zoom to train them. At the promise of a big paycheck, Zoom reluctantly agrees and when it's revealed that the real reason behind the resurrection of the team is because the government discovered Concussion is still alive in another dimension and is plotting his return, Zoom takes it upon himself to make the team ready before his evil brother comes back and puts the planet in jeopardy.

This movie is based on the children's book *Amazing Adventures from Zoom's Academy* by Joe Lethcoe. It's a lighthearted superhero comedy, which is kind of like *X-Men* but with kids and tailored to that audience. Which is totally fine because kids need superhero movies, too, and with the majority of mainstream superhero stuff geared toward adults, I'm glad flicks like this are made.

This flick is chock-full of big names and recognizable faces: Chevy Chase, Rip Torn, Courtney Cox, and, of course, Tim Allen in the lead. Speaking of whom, Tim Allen was pretty funny in this and if you liked him in *Galaxy Quest*, he's pretty much playing the same character of someone who once had glory but has fizzled out. The thing, too, is aside from the funny bits, when it came time to be serious and/or reflective and sad, he nailed it as well and you genuinely felt bad for the guy.

Courtney Cox was the biggest dork in this movie, which was perfect because that was her character. And she played it straight, too, that is, there was no tongue-in-cheek here, but a beautiful nerd that made you love her and roll your eyes at her at the same time.

Chevy Chase—big fan. As the head scientist for Team Zenith, he's just following orders, and with his trademark deadpan humor and wit, I can watch the guy all day.

The kids who made up Team Zenith: just fine. Cute. Funny with kid stuff. The little girl with the superstrength was adorable. The teenager stuff played by actors who were older in real life than their characters— such a Hollywood thing—I could do without, but I hate teenage angst garbage and wish we as a species could just skip those years as we go from kid to grownup. The superpowers displayed were definitely budget: superstrength, telekinetics, invisibility and clairvoyance, and a kid who can blow his body up like a balloon. Yet they worked those not-so-awe-inspiring abilities into the story and made them work for what they needed them to.

I will say that when Captain Zoom cranks up the superspeed later on, it's pretty cool and makes me excited for a Flash movie if it ever happens.

Overall, *Zoom* is a decent flick, good for kids, and if you're a superhero fan it's worth checking out for the sake of a fun time. However, if you're one of those people where everything has to be top notch, then you'll be disappointed.

About the Author

A.P. Fuchs is the author of many novels and short stories. His most recent books are *Canadian Scribbler: Collected Letters of an Underground Writer*, *Redemption of the Dead*, the third book in his zombie trilogy, *Undead World*; *Axiom-man: City of Ruin*; the paranormal romance trilogy, *Blood of my World*; and *Zombie Fight Night: Battles of the Dead*, in which zombies fight such classic monsters as werewolves, vampires, Bigfoot, and even go up against awesome foes like pirates, ninjas, and Bruce Lee. Also a cartoonist, he is known for his superhero series, *The Axiom-man Saga*, both in novel and comic book format.

Please see **www.axiom-man.com** for more on this series. Fuchs's main website is **www.canisterx.com**

THE Axiom-man™ SAGA

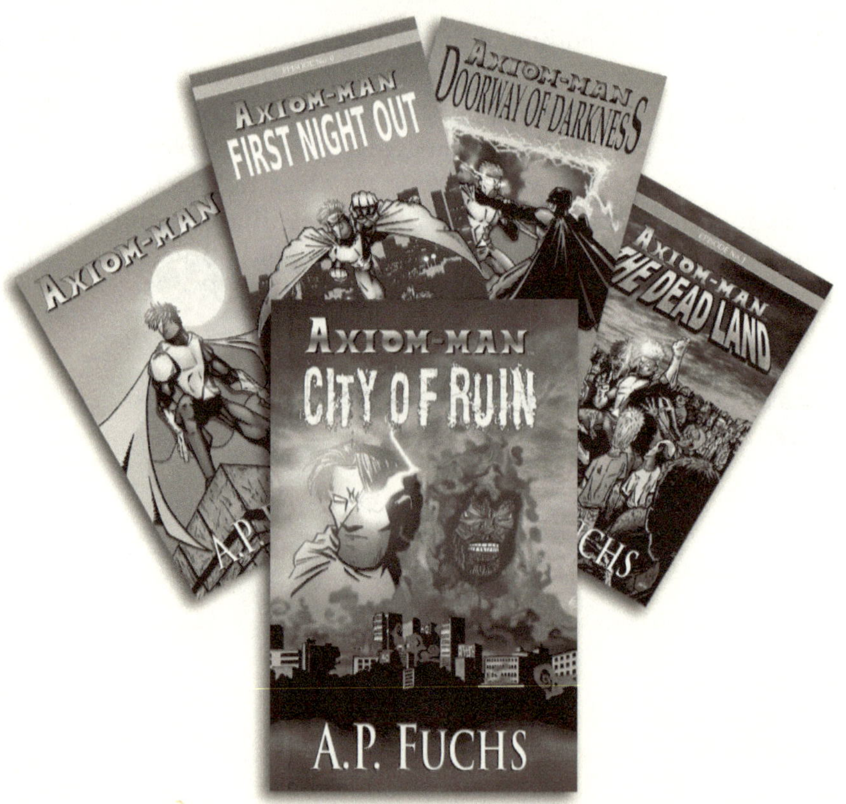

AN ONGOING SUPERHERO BOOK SERIES
BY A.P. FUCHS

Available in paperback and eBook
at your favorite online retailer like Amazon.com

WHAT HAPPENS WHEN METAHUMANS FACE OFF AGAINST THE DEADLIEST FOES?

WELCOME TO THE EXCITING WORLD OF

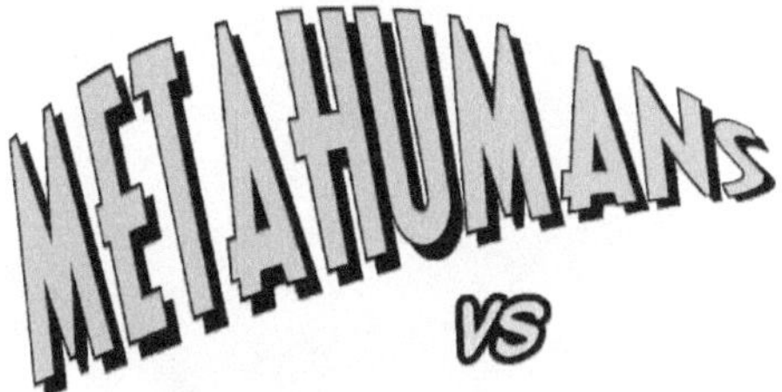

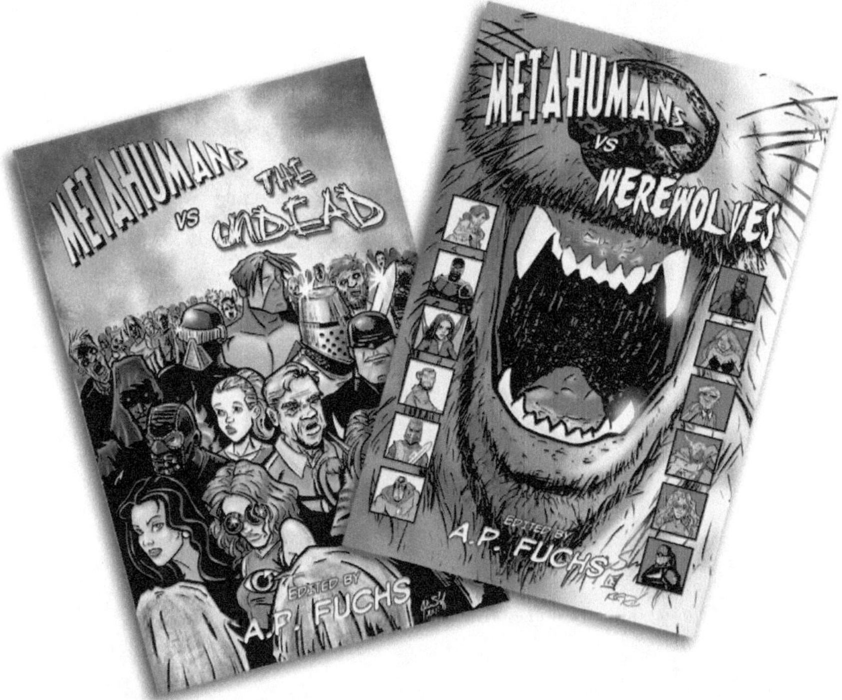

AN ONGOING SUPERHERO ANTHOLOGY SERIES
EDITED BY A.P. FUCHS

Available in paperback and eBook
at your favorite online retailer like Amazon.com

www.ingramcontent.com/pod-product-compliance
Lightning Source LLC
Chambersburg PA
CBHW022046050726
47591CB00002B/411